VICTORIAN WORTHIES

Vanity Fair's Leaders of Church and State

Malcolm Johnson

In affectionate memory of
Roland Macleod
1935–2010

First published in 2014 by
Darton, Longman and Todd Ltd
1 Spencer Court
140 – 142 Wandsworth High Street
London SW1 84JJ

ISBN 978- 0-232-53110-7

A catalogue record for this book is available from the British Library.

Typeset in Great Britain by Kerrypress Ltd, Luton.

Printed and bound by Imak Ofset, Turkey.

Contents

Contents

Acknowledgements

Ian Hislop, editor of *Private Eye* is a direct descendant of Bowles, editor of *Vanity Fair* because both of them use satire and wit to prick the pomposity of the powerful. I am so very grateful to him for writing a Foreword to this book. His appearances for thirty years on *Have I Got News for You* mean that he is the best-known commentator on current issues in the country.

I am grateful to Richard Coles for writing such an affirming postscript. As the regular host of BBC Radio 4's *Saturday Live* programme he speaks to more people than all the clergy put together, and what he says is always interesting and thought-provoking.

Huge thanks also to my friends Kevin Kelly and Paul Thurtle who have helped me by photographing 33 of the caricatures in my collection, and I am grateful to the staff of the Guildhall Library and London Metropolitan Archives for kindly providing the others.

David Moloney, Helen Porter and the staff at DLT have been accessible and supportive and I thank them for the book they have produced.

Foreword by Ian Hislop

Every morning as I stroll to my office at *Private Eye* in Soho I cut through Cecil Court and outside the second-hand bookshops I stop to look at a display of old prints from *Vanity Fair*. This is not just to remind myself in a gloomy way that even the best satirical magazines must pass but because the brilliantly-executed caricatures of Victorian celebrities are still so arresting. Who were these extraordinary figures in their top hats and their frock coats? What was going on in their severe-looking heads and why are they still staring out at me so confidently?

I own a few of these prints now and have the Earl of Shaftesbury up on my wall after I made a documentary about him for a BBC series called *Age of the Do-Gooders*. You will probably recognise the image of Shaftesbury in this book, with its similar but broader theme of 'The Worthies' and there is something very powerful about the drawings, which offer not just a striking likeness but an acute observation of character. I do enjoy the politicians and the lawyers and the actors but I must confess I particularly like the churchmen because in our increasingly secular society it seems so extraordinary that they could once have excited such popular attention. However once you start reading it soon becomes apparent that their lives were well worth the scrutiny.

Malcolm Johnson has done us all a favour by collecting together all the ecclesiastical figures and reproducing the drawings with their original biographies from the magazine. He has then added his own acute observations on their spiritual and earthly lives. The result is a delightful tour of the eccentric, Anglican world of the late nineteenth and early twentieth century. Johnson is a seasoned and entertaining guide to the Church of England and took me expertly through some of its more recent history for a television documentary series called *Canterbury Tales* (Channel 4). He provided an amused yet engaged voice and does the same again here in an even richer territory of political prelates, bachelor bishops, dry deans, litigating nuns, fox-hunting vicars, mad monks and archbishops' lesbian wives ... It is a quite remarkable book. As none of these Victorians probably said at the time, 'Enjoy'.

IAN HISLOP

Introduction

Thomas Gibson Bowles, the editor/owner, founded his magazine in 1868 but it received little attention until he decided to include a weekly caricature, the first of which was Disraeli. This immediately increased the financial wellbeing of *Vanity Fair* and the circulation soared to over 2,500. This momentous decision to introduce 'some Pictorial Wares of an entirely novel character' meant that 2,362 cartoons appeared between 1868 and 1914. I have chosen some of the 104 Anglican clergy who were featured and added other *Worthies* who were devout leaders in the Established Church. Roman Catholics and Nonconformists will have to wait for another volume. In a vignette of around 600 words it is impossible to describe a *Worthy*, so I have listed biographies and reference books to enable further research.

He educated the Tories

Disraeli was drawn by Carlo Pellegrini, 'Ape', aged 25, who had arrived in London in November 1864 and been taken up by the Prince of Wales and his set who commissioned him to sketch them.[1] Bowles soon realised that Pellegrini's ability to 'charge and exaggerate such lines and tones as exist already' in the faces and figures of his famous victims, was just what was needed.

Leslie Ward, 'Spy', a youth of 22, was introduced to Bowles by Millais in 1873 and he produced over 1,300 cartoons for the magazine. He relished his position as a sketcher of Society and was probably too sympathetic to his subjects. However, today he is still famous and all *Vanity Fair* caricatures are often known as 'Spy cartoons'.

The caricature was followed on the next page by a biographical commentary written by Bowles, under the pseudonym *Jehu Junior*. Often they were polished, witty and as amusing as the cartoon. Bowles had no staff only contributors, who remained anonymous and sent their comments to his smart office in St James's Street. There were no boozy, weekly lunches.

Private Eye's 'Bishop of the Month' caused much merriment in the 1990s. They were often scandalous, incisive and revealing. I was, however, told that some bishops were very offended that they were not featured. The same happened in *Vanity Fair* because Bowles excluded those he disliked, including Dickens.

I have collected the caricatures since the early 1960s when they cheered up the church history lectures at Cuddesdon Theological College. Many were purchased from Mr Bloch's delightfully Dickensian shop in Barter Street, Bloomsbury where he sat in the far corner of a large room with a huge centre table piled high with

---

[1] The drawings are preserved in the Royal Library at Windsor.

folders. His wife, who sat by the door, told us not to buy anything because 'his prices are too high'.

Each week the magazine treated its readers to a lively and often libellous burlesque on contemporary political 'vanities' and the shape of its contents remained much the same. Its size and format - eight to twelve folio pages including advertisements, a commentary on the week's political and social events, reviews, features on finance, the church and law – were popular from the start. Its tone was 'light, epigrammatic, pungent and excessively neat'.[2] The adverts, for wines, cheeses, cigars, ladies' dresses and gloves, pain remedies and resort hotels reveal that the readership was middle and upper class. Society news and gossip rubbed shoulders with Parliamentary debates and regular features such as word games and book reviews.

The 'Bible' for this subject is Matthews and Mellini's *In 'Vanity Fair'* which gives details of all the caricatures. The judges, jockeys, cricketers and doctors[3] have their books, so now I add the ecclesiastics.

The *Worthies* are not so far away as we might think. I have met one - Churchill in 1951, and have an autograph to prove it. Also I was ordained by a bishop who was consecrated by a bishop who was consecrated by a bishop who was consecrated by Samuel Wilberforce. The actor Roland Macleod, to whom this book is dedicated, worked that one out. He had the best training a thespian can

---

[2] Journalist, *Bohemian Days in Fleet Street*, p.70.
[3] R Collens, *25 Legal Luminaries from 'Vanity Fair'* (1990); Alan Sykes, *The Doctors of 'Vanity Fair'* (2003) ; Russell March, *The Cricketers of 'Vanity Fair'* (1993) and Russell March, *The Jockeys of 'Vanity Fair'* (1985).

have – nearly two years at a theological college – and he specialised in clerical roles. He was the vicar in *Coronation Street*, and sadly he died in 2010.

These write-ups are no longer accessible to the general reader, and the original drawings are very difficult to find indeed. However, prints of the cartoons are available today for sums varying from £15 to £300.

In 1884 Bowles became proprietor of a new journal, *The Lady*, which still exists. His interest in *Vanity Fair* waned and in March 1899 he sold it to Arthur Evans for £20,000, (£2.1 million in 2012 prices). In 1914 the magazine was absorbed by *Hearth and Home*.

As will be seen by the 50 caricatures with commentaries which follow Bowles could be kind – or caustic. Henry Villiers, Vicar of St Paul Knightsbridge in 1902 was described as:

> Not very beautiful to look at, but there is no better persuader of money out of ladies' pockets. He is a splendid beggar.[4]

Harvey Goodwin, Bishop of Carlisle:

> … exemplifies the truth that earnestly delivered platitudes often obtain weight and command attention. He is an excellent, undistinguished, second class Bishop.

Ryle, the evangelical Bishop of Liverpool is:

---

[4] Married to Lady Victoria Russell, daughter of the Prime Minister; they had 10 children.

… a great favourite with women; he is fond of exercise, fresh air and matrimony, and has been married three times. He is a good man, not at all large-minded, but very much in earnest.

Bishop Colenso of Natal:

was called by many hard names and since it was found that he could not be refuted, it was resolved that he should be prayed for in the next world and ruined in this.

David Maclagan   Edward Bickersteth

David Maclagan, Archbishop of York (1891–1908), reminds us of a Bishop of Worcester of the 1970s:

The Queen has shown favour to his second wife;[5] of which fact his new Deacons have been generally made aware by kindly invitation into his drawing room, where it has been permitted to them to inspect the album which incloses a letter of congratulation over the signature 'Victoria'.

Bickersteth, is a very great man in the Church. He obtained a large number of those youthful honours which to Churchmen signify so much and to others so little. A gentle, impartial and inflexible Prolocutor of the Convocation of Canterbury. Despite his years he is as young as ever. He has never made an enemy or lost a friend. He married at 68.

Where would Ward and Bowles find their ecclesiastics in today's dull and drab Church of England? Rowan Williams, Richard Chartres and John Sentamu would make splendid caricatures and are obvious choices, as are Donald Reeves, Roger Royle (the secretary of whose fan club lives at the end of the Mall), and former Communard Richard Coles. Michael Marshall is a latter-day Edward King. Deans are a dreary lot but Victor Stock formerly of Guildford and June Osborne of Salisbury would be suitable - provided she brings her young Bishop with her. Famous, holy laity are hard to find, but Ian Hislop, A. N. Wilson and Roy Strong (provided he wears his Abbey outfit) are candidates. Who else?

---

[5] The Hon Augusta Anne Barrington, a granddaughter of the 6th Viscount Barrington.

The 50 caricatures in the following pages appear in the order they were published in *Vanity Fair*. On the page following each caricature we have printed, in bold, the caption that appeared beneath the original illustration, and, in italic, Bowles' original commentary.

MALCOLM JOHNSON

1

William Ewart Gladstone (1809–1898)

Ape's cartoon of the Prime Minister, 6 February 1869

'Were he a worse man, he would be a better statesman'

The merits he possesses are so great that the only defects imputed to him are such as spring from their very excess. A mind so vast as to be almost universal enables him at once to grasp the smallest and meanest details and the largest principles. A fearless intellect content to rely upon pure reason for its conclusions ... a sense of justice, so intense as to be insatiable, leads him to open his mind to every view of every subject ... a genuine enthusiasm for the right, which knows no bounds, makes him passionate in its defence and eager for its triumph.

Gladstone appeared nine times in *Vanity Fair* and had just become PM when the first cartoon (above) was published – tall, prominent nose, piercing gaze, stern look; he knows that he is right. A political contemporary observed that he had a habit of concealing the ace of trumps up his sleeve, and claiming that God had put it there.[1] Jehu, although not a political supporter, reluctantly admired him. When Gladstone was born the vast majority of the British people lived and died in conditions of appalling misery. Thanks to his extraordinary sense of Christian mission and to the work of others such as Dickens, Kingsley and Shaftesbury all that was to change.

---

[1]   R. Matthews and P. Mellini, *In Vanity Fair* (1982), p. 55.

His mother was an Evangelical and taught her son to pray daily and attend church twice on Sundays. He avidly read theological books and gradually turned to a more High Church viewpoint although he disliked ritualism. At one point he considered ordination.

The son of a Liverpool merchant, Gladstone went to Eton then Christ Church Oxford and entered the Commons as Tory MP for Newark in 1832. Peel liked him and made him Colonial Secretary. Twice he was Chancellor of the Exchequer, then became Prime Minister in 1868 and served four terms, a total of 12 years.

In 1848 he founded the Church Penitentiary Association for the Reclamation of Fallen Women, and in May 1849 he began his most active 'rescue work' and met prostitutes late at night on the street, in his house or in their houses, writing their names in a private notebook. There is no evidence that he ever acted in an improper way with these women.

Gladstone's influence on choosing bishops was immense. His secretary, Edward Hamilton commented, 'A vacant See is a great excitement to Mr G. Indeed I believe it excites him far more than a political crisis'. Disraeli, who said that GOM stood not for Great Old Man but 'God's only mistake', pondered a man's politics; whereas Gladstone wanted a bishop to be pious, learned, administratively competent and eloquent. Victoria always treated him with coolness ('He addresses me like a public meeting') and in 1897 when they met in Cannes she shook his hand – for the first time according to him.

Having read over 20,000 books he pronounced with great moral force on the issues of the day, and he had prodigious energy; chopping trees down was a pastime. Roy Jenkins, his biographer, describes him as a 'compelling orator who, despite his addiction to endless sentences, convoluted constructions, and classical allusion and quotation, could hold the House of Commons and popular audiences transfixed for hours at a time. He was always the biggest beast in the forest and he had inherent star quality'.[2]

'The People's William' died on 19 May 1898 at Hawarden Castle, Hawarden, aged 88. He was given a state funeral at Westminster Abbey, at which the Prince of Wales (the future Edward VII) and the Duke of York (the future George V) acted as pallbearers. Two years after Gladstone's burial in Westminster Abbey, his wife, Catherine, by whom he had eight children, was laid to rest with him.

[2] Roy Jenkins, *Gladstone* (1995), pp. xiv, xv.

Mrs Star

Ape caricatures the former Mother Superior,
20 February 1869

'I felt very uncomfortable'

The case against Star was heard before Lord Chief Justice Cockburn on 3 February 1869 and caused a furore in the country. So much so that the caricature of her was, with Gladstone and Disraeli, one of the first four printed in the magazine. As Mother Superior of a Roman Catholic convent in Hull she was accused by a former nun of the community, Susan Saurin, of assault on divers occasions, and conspiring to drive her from the convent. Miss Saurin, formerly Sister Mary Scholastica Joseph, alleged that Sister Mary Joseph (Mrs Star) and another nun beat her, deprived her of food and clothing, prevented her from attending services and kept family letters from her. Indeed, passages of those given to her were blotted out, and she was not told that her father was ill. Because of all this *'she was rendered sick and ill and greatly distressed in body and mind'*.

The Solicitor General, who represented Saurin, said that the facts were 'strange and painful as a revelation of female nature, and particularly of conventual female nature, showing what women are capable of when they shut themselves up from their kind ... and what mean and petty cruelties they can wreak upon their sisters, and that under the supposed sanction of religion'.

The two women had joined the Sisters of Mercy in 1851, then moved to Hull where there were only seven sisters. Mrs Star told the court that Saurin was dissatisfied with, and complains of, her boots and shoes and the food given to her. 'She is late in her duties and eats during the hours when it is prohibited.' The letters to her family were too tender and affectionate; one beginning 'My ever dearest uncle' was deemed excessive. Then there was Saurin's 'great forwardness' in her relationship with a local priest. Mrs Star had a feeling that all was not right. The priest had been 'completely deceived' about Saurin's real character, and when he described her as a saint of the community it made Mrs Star feel 'very uncomfortable'. 'I observed she put herself constantly and needlessly in his way, sought to attract his notice by various little acts, talked to him frequently'. Mrs Star said Saurin was worldly and had a fondness of clothes. She was unwilling to teach in the school and stole the children's food. The Bishop had appointed a Commission to investigate the situation which after hearing evidence expelled her from the convent in 1865.

On her part Saurin said that Mrs Star had in 1861 asked what had happened when she made her confession and she had declined to answer. From that moment 'the demeanour of the Mother Superior was changed towards her'.

Anti-Catholicism was rife in England at this time despite recent liberal legislation, so the trial, with its description of what lies behind convent walls and clerical collars, fuelled the fire. Every day the courtroom in Westminster Hall was packed, and proceedings were given much press publicity. Each morning crowds gathered including many nuns and priests to queue for a seat.[1] The local paper observed that a young girl 'would do well to pause' before entering a convent if the testimony given in court was indicative of how she would be treated'.[2]

Miss Saurin asked for £5,000 damages, and on 26 February the jury decided in favour of Saurin and awarded her £500 (approx £47,000 today). Cheers were heard outside the courtroom. The defendants appealed, and two months later agreed to an out-of-court settlement.

Ape's caricature of Mrs Star, with her 'furtive glance, down-turned mouth, clasped hands and hunched shoulders hints that she was not free of guilt'.[3]

[1] Roy Matthews and Peter Mellini, p. 126.
[2] *The Eastern Morning News and Hull Advertiser*, 6 February 1869.
[3] Matthews and Mellini, p.127.

3
William Page Wood, Baron Hatherley (1801–1881)

Ape's caricature, 20 March 1869

'When He Who Has Too Little Piety is Impossible, and He Who Has Too Much is Impracticable; He Who Has Equal Piety and Ability Becomes Lord Chancellor'

In a Government of which the distinguishing principle is a tempered Radicalism, it is both natural and appropriate that the Keeper of the Queen's conscience should be an amiable Radical religionist.

That his Radicalism is incontestable is sufficiently proved by the fact that he was one of the strongest advocates of the ballot as long as twenty years ago when it was regarded with almost universal horror; while, as a religionist, he is so earnest that one sex alone is inadequate to supply the missionaries he desires to see at work, and that he would supplement male logic by female persuasion for the propagation of truth. He has piety and ability

Wood was the second son of the Lord Mayor of London Sir Matthew Wood who befriended Queen Caroline and thus risked the wrath of George IV. As a senior prefect he was expelled from Winchester College in 1818 for his involvement in a protest against a master who had beaten prefects. After Geneva University and Trinity College Cambridge he entered Lincoln's Inn and was called to the bar in 1827, becoming a QC 20 years later. In 1830 he married Charlotte Moore and until 1844 they lived in Dean's Yard, Westminster. They had no children.

A strong high-church man and an advanced Liberal, he entered Parliament in 1847 representing Oxford, and spoke mainly on ecclesiastical topics such as supporting church rates, the admission of Jews to Parliament, and the Ecclesiastical Commission. In 1849 its members asked him to sit on the splendidly-named Episcopal and Capitular Revenues Commission which had to decide how church lands could be rendered most productive and beneficial 'with due regard to the present holders of the property'. Needless to say the tenants were vocal and in the bill brought to Parliament Page Wood, then solicitor-general, won them over by inserting the magic words 'just and reasonable claims'. Colonel Sibthorp, their leader, wanted the bill passed quickly because 'what with grouse shooting approaching, and Goodwood races on, and other amusements' time was short. The Act was passed.[1]

He supported the anti-Catholic Ecclesiastical Titles Bill of 1851 which unsuccessfully attempted to stop Roman Catholic bishops taking the titles of a city or town. Having been vice-chancellor he was made Lord Chancellor by Gladstone in 1868, and became Baron Hatherley. Because of very poor eyesight his judgements were oral rather than written. He was not an eloquent speaker but played an effective part in the debate on the Irish Church. *His place will be won in the House of Lords by his advocacy of the abolition of a branch of the very Church of which he is so strong a supporter.*

Hatherley stayed in touch with his school-friend Walter Hook and was instrumental in his appointment to the incumbency of Leeds, and then to the Deanery of

---

[1]   GFA Best, *Temporal Pillars* (1964), pp. 378 – 9.

Chichester where he contributed to the success of the Dean's appeal to repair the cathedral.

A deeply pious man, from 1834 he was on the committee of the National Society and was a Sunday School teacher at St Margaret Westminster for over 40 years.[2] His two successors, Cairns and Selborne, were also Sunday School teachers, which is surprising as before 1870 many thought that these teachers were 'half-educated and narrow-minded' and the classes 'a disorderly bear garden'.[3] In 1877 Randall Davidson in a letter said that he considered Hatherley 'one of the finest specimens of a Christian man of genius I have ever seen'.[4] Lord Westbury described him as 'a mere bundle of virtues without a redeeming vice'. Tolerant and devout, he disapproved of any religion-based political disability.

Nearly blind he retired in 1872 but continued hearing appeals to the Judicial Committee of the Privy Council. He died nine years later, and was buried in the churchyard of Great Bealings, Suffolk beside his wife. Her brother was the rector.

[2]   DNB vol. 60, J. A. Hamilton, p.152.
[3]   Owen Chadwick, *The Victorian Church Part 2* (1970), p. 258.
[4]   G. K. A. Bell, *Randall Davidson* vol. 1 (1935), p. 40.

The Earl of Derby (1799–1869)

Ape's caricature of the former Prime Minister,
29 May 1869

'It is His Mission to Stem the Tide of Democracy'

Lord Derby is not the best leader that the aristocracy has had in this country by any means. He is too far removed by fortune from the sway of the more sordid influences which have developed so many great men, to regard anything very seriously. Lord Derby is a great orator, but he is essentially juvenile in all his thoughts and acts; he does all things as a boy. The lightness of character and conviction has done him no great harm as a leader, but it has irretrievably damaged the cause of which he has been the champion, and there may yet be room to ask whether, after having passed the Household Suffrage Bill, it can still be said of him as he once said of himself, that it is his mission to stem the tide of Democracy.

Derby was Prime Minister for three brief periods – eleven months in 1852 and three years between 1858 and 1868. Born into the wealthy and aristocratic Derby family (the Epsom horse race was named after his grandfather), he was educated at Eton where Pusey recalled that he displayed 'an iron will and an unbounded self-confidence'.   At Christ Church Oxford he led a group of drunk undergrads who pulled down a statue in the Great Quadrangle. He entered the Commons as a Whig in 1821, but switched to the Tories, becoming Peel's Colonial Secretary in 1841. He succeeded to the earldom in 1851.

Edward Stanley, as he then was, was a devout man, had a private chapel in his house and regularly attended worship.

When Stanley first became Prime Minister the Prince Consort was worried that he belonged to the fast racing set who would allot plums at Court to 'the Dandies and Roués of London and the Turf' so lectured him about immorality. The days of Melbourne who considered 'damned morality would undo us all' were over. Balmorality had arrived. The lecture must have worked because soon afterwards Victoria wrote that Derby was 'most attentive, fluent and clear'.

Derby returned to power with Disraeli as a leading figure in his Cabinet, for the third and last time in 1866. This administration was particularly notable for the passage of the Reform Act of 1867 which greatly expanded the suffrage. Although a great orator, Derby was frequently criticised for his languid leadership and aloofness. His tenure of 22 years as party leader still stands as the longest in Conservative Party history. His attractive tenor voice, precise diction, clearness of style and great intelligence made him an effective speaker, but before a speech, he told a friend, 'I am like a man about to be hanged'. When asked why heaven is like a bald head he did not give the usual reply 'both are shining places where no parting exists', but said, 'In neither place is a Whig in sight'.

The gouty Derby's health deteriorated and in 1868, the year before his death, he decided to retire and hand over to Disraeli, but he was hurt by the Queen's curt letter. His son noted, 'She is civil to persons in power

under her whose good will contributes to her comfort ...
but sees no reason for wasting civility on those who can
no longer be of use to her'.[1]

Aged 70 he died at Knowsley Hall Lancashire, his
family seat, and was buried in St Mary's church there.

[1]   Bernard Palmer, *High and Mitred* (1992), pp. 62 – 66.

Earl Russell (1792–1878)

Ape's caricature of the 77 year old former PM,
5 June 1869

'The Greatest Liberal Statesman of Modern Times'

Lord John Russell was only 5ft 4ins tall and eight stone, so Pellegrini depicts him sitting on the benches of the Lords with his feet far from the floor. Sydney Smith commented that before the start of the Reform Act crisis, Russell was 'over six feet high, but, engaged in looking after your interests, fighting the peers, the landlords and the rest of your natural enemies, he has been so constantly kept in hot water that he is boiled down to the proportions in which you now behold him'.

As the youngest son of the 6th Duke of Bedford he was born into one of the greatest Whig dynasties and was known as Lord John Russell until his elevation. He entered Westminster School in 1803 but it was 'too much' for him and he had a tutor at home until he went to Edinburgh University.

He had sympathy for the poor, and aged 14 remarked 'What a pity that he who steals a penny loaf should be hung, whilst he who steals thousands of the public money should be acquitted'.

He was a Liberal by conviction when to be such was a reproach, and he carried out his principles when to do so was almost a crime. He was the author of the repeal of the Test and Corporation Acts and of the first Reform Bill and with consummate ability carried them through. Nevertheless he never enjoyed popularity and the reason is that he has never bowed the knee to the potentates of the press

A Whig, he was the first Liberal Premier (1846–52) and was thoroughly imbued with the optimism that was a hallmark of the Victorian Liberal outlook; as Sydney Smith remarked, 'I believe he would perform the operation for a stone or build St Peter's or assume (with or without ten minutes' notice) the command of the Channel Fleet; and no one would discover by his manner that the patient had died – the Church tumbled down – and the Channel Fleet been knocked to atoms'.[1]

In 1813 he became MP for the family borough of Tavistock; he was one of a four man committee who prepared the Reform Bill and helped to guide it through Parliament despite opposition particularly from the House of Lords - 168 constituencies were to disappear. On 12 December 1831 Lord John introduced the third Reform Bill, which received Royal Assent the following June.

On 20 July 1841, Lord John married Lady Fanny Elliot, daughter of the second earl of Minto, and they had four children.

Russell became Prime Minister on 28 June 1846 and appointed Professor Hampden to be Bishop of Hereford which caused a furore. Bishop Phillpotts shrieked, 'Persist not in your rash experiment.'[2]

---

[1]   Hesketh Pearson *The Smith of Smiths* (1934) p. 284.
[2]   G.P. Gooch (ed.), *The Later Correspondence of Lord John Russell 1840–1878* vol 1, p. 184.

Russell was a religious man, and attended church services regularly. The Hampden affair taught Russell to be more cautious about his patronage in the future. He remained firmly anti-Tractarian, probably because of the Papal Aggression of 1850 whereby the Pope had created dioceses in England. Russell told the Bishop of Durham that a greater danger came from ministers of the Established Church who were 'step by step leading their flocks to the verge of the precipice'. Accordingly he made sure that no Tractarian reached the Bench. Anti-ritualist riots continued at Russell's own church of St Barnabas Pimlico, and some felt Russell himself was partly to blame.

Russell's voice was 'small and thin', his pronunciation was archaic, and he scarcely knew, when speaking, where 'to dispose of his hands or feet'. But 'there was something manly and even vigorous in his bearing'.[3]

He died in 1878, aged 86, and is buried in the family vault at Chenies, Buckinghamshire. Gladstone succeeded him as Liberal leader.

[3] John Prest, 'John first Earl Russell (1792–1878)', *Oxford Dictionary of National Biography*, http://www.oxforddnb.com/view/article/24325.

6

The Marquis of Salisbury (1830–1903)

Ape's portrait, 10 July 1869

'He is Too Honest a Tory for His Party and His Time'

When in these times a politician allows his principles to run away with him, we usually smile and pity him, even if the principles are the greatest and grandest that exist; and the less great and grand they are the more we smile and the less we pity ... He believes that pure Tory principles have still life and strength enough to form a creed that will suffice for the purposes of a party. He believes it with passionate earnestness, and therefore it is that he so hates and despises those of his party who wiser, if not more respectable, in their generation, have long since abandoned any such notion. His incisive argument and biting sarcasm are henceforth for ever directed against such traitors as these seem to him to be.

Lord Robert Cecil, as he was styled until 1865, was a direct descendant of Elizabeth I's ministers Lord Burghley and Robert Cecil. He was born at Hatfield House, Hertfordshire, on 3 February 1830, the fifth of six children. He had a passionate temper and was a solitary and sensitive child who was bullied so badly at Eton (where he showed an unusual aptitude for theology), that he was withdrawn from the school, but in 1847 went up to Christ Church, Oxford. Tall, thin, stooped, shy and deplorably dressed, depression and ill health dogged his early life but this changed when in 1857 he married Georgina Alderson, daughter of the judge Sir

Edward Alderson. She shared his intellectual interests and encouraged and facilitated his career; they had five sons and three daughters

He entered the Commons in 1853 as MP for Stamford. In 1867, after his brother Eustace complained of being addressed by constituents in a hotel, Cecil responded: 'A hotel infested by influential constituents is worse than one infested by bugs. It's a pity you can't carry around a powder insecticide to get rid of vermin of that kind'.[1]

As Viscount Cranborne, he resigned from Disraeli's government because of a Bill which extended the county franchise to householders rated at £12 annually. On 15 July1867 the third reading of the Bill took place and he spoke first, in a speech which his biographer Andrew Roberts has called 'possibly the greatest oration of a career full of powerful parliamentary speeches'.

Salisbury was a devout churchman who took immense pains over ecclesiastical appointments – there seemed to be a high episcopal mortality during his time – 'I declare they die to spite me' he said. A total of 38 diocesan mitres were given by him. He commented, 'I wish all Bishops were appointed like the Apostle Mathias, by lot'.

---

[1] Andrew Roberts, *Salisbury* (1999), p. 21.

6 continued ....

The Prime Minister

The Marquis of Salisbury
Spy's caricature of Salisbury, 20 December 1900

The Marquis of Salisbury

He is very little known outside a small circle. He has filled
many Great Offices with much dignity, he is full of experience
and learning ... he is an able master of cynicism who can say
very nasty things like a gentleman. His virtues indeed are
very many; and his great fault (in these democratic days)
is his capacity for ignoring the views of that person who has
come to be known as the Man in the Street. He is probably
the most brilliant of the ten Prime Ministers who have served
the Queen – he is a shy man who lives a secluded life.

The General Election of 1886 returned Salisbury to
the Premiership for the last time, and this lasted, with
one break of nearly three years, for 16 years. Victoria's
satisfaction was profound that Gladstone had gone,
and she at last abandoned her seclusion. Parliamentary
reform was raised in the mid-1860s, but Cecil argued
that working men should not be given an electoral
preponderance overwhelming the voice of other classes
of society.

Salisbury's expertise was in foreign affairs. For most
of his time as Prime Minister he also served as Foreign
Secretary and pursued a policy of splended isolation,
although British troops fought in the Boer War from
October 1899 until May 1902. The death of Victoria in
1901 was a personal blow to Salisbury; he remembered
her coronation and had a good working relationship,
even friendship, with her, and he was accorded the rare
privilege of sitting during his audiences with her. 'She is

very fond of him' said Violet, his daughter-in-law, 'I never saw two people get on better'.[2]

Salisbury was twice offered a dukedom by the Queen but declined because of the financial cost. On 11 July 1902, in failing health and broken hearted over the death of his wife, Salisbury resigned, and was succeeded by his nephew, Arthur Balfour. ('Bob's your uncle.') Salisbury died at Hatfield House on 22 August 1903 surrounded by his family. Having refused an Abbey interment, he was buried at Hatfield on 31 August.

[2] Roberts, p. 793.

7

Samuel Wilberforce (1805–73)

Ape's cartoon of the Bishop of Oxford, 24 July 1869

'Not a Brawler'

It is not for nothing that he is descended from the philanthropic Wilberforce, for he shows in all he does and says that he loves his fellow men and women in a much more attractive and less impractical way than is usual among bishops.

He is not a brawler but goes beyond this, and is an adept in the graceful social arts which are even more efficacious than sermons in making life pleasant; so that if the English Church was disestablished tomorrow he assuredly would be provided for by a grateful country as the most amusing diner-out of his time.

Jehu obviously respected Wilberforce but describes him as a lightweight which he certainly was not. In 1868 if Archbishop Longley had lived another two months Gladstone not Disraeli would have been Prime Minister, and it is highly likely that Wilberforce would have gone to London or Canterbury, although Gladstone would have had to convince the Queen who regarded Soapy Sam with suspicion for being a Tractarian. As it was, he was given Winchester and remained there until he died.

Various explanations are given for his nickname; he himself said there were many times when he was in hot water but he always emerged with clean hands. Others remember Disraeli's comment that the Bishop's manner was 'unctuous, oleaginous and saponaceous'.

Samuel Wilberforce

Samuel was the third son of William Wilberforce and was brought up in the devout evangelical household on Clapham Common. At Oriel College he met many Oxford men including Gladstone and Manning and became known for his liberal views. Ordained in 1828 he did a curacy at Henley followed by incumbencies in the Isle of Wight then Alverstoke, Hampshire. A High Churchman, he did not associate with the Tractarians, and in 1845 Sir Robert Peel made him Bishop of Oxford with Victoria's approval because Sam was one of Prince Albert's chaplains. Bishop Blomfield was one of his greatest supporters and hoped that he might follow him at London.

Like many Victorians Sam knew the meaning of sorrow. In 1841 his beloved wife Emily died giving birth to their fourth son, and he threw himself into his work. His loneliness was also compounded by a sense of isolation as, one by one, those closest to him joined the Roman Catholic Church – his three brothers, his daughter, and Manning.

He made Oxford with its 600 parishes a model diocese and was a familiar figure in the wider Church - he was one of the best preachers in England. He founded a seminary next to his Palace at Cuddesdon which has produced many bishops and competent clergy (including the author!), and a college for teachers was founded nearby at Culham. He and Henry Philpotts of Exeter were the only diocesan bishops who sanctioned the new Religious Orders for women.[1]

[1] See Valerie Bonham, *A Place in Life* (1992).

For many people today Wilberforce is remembered for his legendary encounter on 30 June 1860 in Oxford with Thomas Huxley to argue publicly the case for and against Darwin's theory of evolution by natural selection; Darwin was too ill to be present so Huxley was his 'bulldog'. The Bishop enjoyed banter and in a *Natural History Review* article had lampooned Darwin's ideas of 'our unsuspected cousinship with mushrooms'. Now 700 people at a British Association meeting heard Sam, a Fellow of the Royal Society, go on the attack, criticising Darwin's theory on scientific grounds arguing that it was not supported by the facts and many great scientists did not accept it. He then asked Huxley whether he was descended from the apes through his grandmother or grandfather. Huxley replied that he saw no reason to be ashamed of having an ape for an ancestor. 'If there were an ancestor whom I should feel shame in recalling, it would rather be a *man* – a man of restless and versatile intellect – who, not content with success in his own sphere of activity, plunges into scientific questions with which he has no real acquaintance, only to obscure them by an aimless rhetoric.[2] Uproar followed and one lady fainted. Sam thought that he had won the day but others disagreed. Everyone, however, went off cheerfully together to enjoy a good dinner.

In 1873 Wilberforce fell when his horse stumbled, and he died instantly. The family declined the offer of a Westminster Abbey interment and he was buried next to his wife at the family churchyard in Lavington on 25 July.

---

[2] Standish Meacham, *Lord Bishop* (1970), p.216.

After his death Victoria wrote to Gladstone: 'The Queen admired and liked him *most before* he became a Bishop, and before he leant so much to those High Church views which did harm'.[3] This may explain why the highest offices evaded Sam.

8

Frederick Temple (1821–1902)

Coide's caricature of the new Bishop of Exeter,
6 November 1869

'He Has Displayed Ability in the Free Handling of Religious Subjects, and Has Nevertheless Been Made a Bishop'

His enemies say he is destitute of the abilities and qualities that a Bishop should have. In his present job he has won respect and love. He describes himself as 'an old cab horse: all right so long as I'm in the shafts'.

The Temple family lived in Devon so he was sent to Blundell's School in Tiverton and from there, before he was 17, he won a scholarship to Balliol College, Oxford. In 1842 he took a double first and was elected a fellow of Balliol, and lecturer in mathematics and logic. Four years later he was ordained by Samuel Wilberforce, became a school-inspector and in 1858 was appointed Headmaster of Rugby School. Prince Albert thought highly of him and he became a chaplain to the Queen. His tremendous powers of work and rough manner intimidated the pupils. (One said, 'He *is* a beast but he is a Just Beast'.)

At the age of 55 Temple married Beatrice Lascelles, and he 'renewed his youth' by being with their two sons, one of whom, William, would follow his father to Canterbury. Temple's interest in education meant that when the Education Act, 1870 was passed he was anxious that church schools should not lag behind the new State schools, and he raised funds to ensure this did not happen.

After 16 years Temple was translated to London, and at his confirmation in St Mary-le-Bow there were protests, because he was a believer in evolution. He was much concerned with the social ills of the Capital, and considered intemperance the biggest single social evil of the time. He spoke in the Lords on this subject hoping for stricter legislation, and he encouraged the clergy to help form public opinion against alcohol.[1]

When Benson died the Queen hoped that Randall Davidson would be his successor as Archbishop, but Lord Salisbury wanted Temple even though he was 76. 'He is far too advanced to undertake such an arduous position' said the Queen who was two years older than Temple. However, Victoria agreed and Davidson had to wait. Simple and austere, Temple's best work had already been done, but for six years he threw himself into the job with characteristic enthusiasm.

The Lambeth Conference of 1897 was chaired by the Archbishop who was firm, perhaps too much so. He told one loquacious prelate 'next time you don't want others to talk, keep your own mouth shut', and to another 'what you mean is all right, but what you say isn't what you mean'.[2] The bishops set up a consultative committee to supply information and advice to them in the intervening years, and this still exists. Austere and abrupt, Temple found it difficult to delegate and this caused problems toward the end of his life.

---

[1] Edward Carpenter, *Cantuar* (1971), pp. 397 – 8.
[2] *Ibid.* p. 396.

The death of Victoria in 1901 meant that the Archbishop, now 81, had to preside at Edward VII's Coronation the following year despite what Davidson called his 'tottering gait' and near blindness. In the event his words were printed in large type on scrolls and these were unrolled one by one. Mistakes were made because these were not held firmly.[3] He put the crown on the King's head back to front and when he knelt to pay homage he was unable to get up, and had to be helped to his feet by the King who kissed his hand. 'Go away' rasped Temple to Davidson who asked him how he was. He died four months later and was interred in Canterbury Cathedral.

[3] Roy Strong, *Coronation* (2005), p.475.

9

The Earl of Shaftesbury (1801–1885)

Ape's cartoon, 13 November 1869

'He is not as other men are, for he is never influenced by party motives'

Lord Shaftesbury's name is one which must ever be dear to the religious and philanthropic few who are the shining lights of this dark country. Whenever evangelical views are to be vindicated to the discomfiture of all others, he is the chosen champion; whenever there is the smallest project for effecting the most microscopic improvement in the condition of pious labourers, he is always ready to suggest refinements and improvements upon the original scheme ... Charity does not in him, as in too many others, overlie Consistency. There are not wanting those who call Lord Shaftesbury's piety sanctimonious, his philanthropy foolish, and his consistency bigoted.

Anthony Ashley Cooper, known as Lord Ashley until 1851 when he became the 7th Earl of Shaftesbury, was educated at Harrow School and Christ Church, Oxford. He grew up without any experience of parental love. He saw little of his parents, and when duty or necessity compelled them to take notice of him they were formal and frightening. This difficult childhood was softened by the affection he received from his housekeeper Maria Millis, and his sisters. As Best, his biographer, explains: 'What did touch him was the reality, and the homely practicality, of the love which her Christianity made her feel towards the unhappy child'.[1]

He entered Parliament as a Tory MP in 1826 and almost immediately became the leader of many reform movements including those working towards the Factory Acts, the Ten Hours Bill, the Mines and Collieries Act, the Lunacy Act and various Bills for children's welfare. He was chairman of the Ragged Schools Union.

His marriage to Lady Emily (Minnie) Cowper brought important political connections as she was probably the illegitimate daughter of Lord Palmerston, and her maternal uncle was Lord Melbourne. It was a happy marriage and produced ten children. Ashley was a wily politician who knew all the tricks of the parliamentary trade, and his family connection with Palmerston gave him considerable influence during the two periods Palmerston was Prime Minister; not just support for social reforms but also for ecclesiastical appointments. There were 19 men to be found for bishoprics in 1855–8 and 1859–65, and Shaftesbury soon became the chief, and often the only advisor. According to him the Prime Minister knew little of theology – 'he does not know Moses from Sydney Smith'. [2] He told the Queen that 'much mischief has been done by theological bishops'.

Owen Chadwick notes that 'the profession of evangelical opinion had until this moment erected a fence against preferment. In February 1855 the fence collapsed and reappeared as a ladder'.

---

[1] G.F.A. Best, *Shaftesbury* (1964), pp. 14,15.
[2] J. Ridley, *Lord Palmerston* (1970), pp 499 – 500.

Queen Victoria did not care for Ashley and declined to support his Ten Hours Bill which would limit the hours of workers, many of whom were children, in mills and factories. This, she thought, would deprive industry of seven weeks' child-power each year and thus make England less competitive in the world market.

The professor of Latin at University College, London, J.R. Seeley, published *Ecce Homo* in 1865, and in a throwaway remark Shaftesbury described it as the 'most pestilential book ever vomited from the jaws of Hell'. Seeley was delighted and later reported that sales shot up by 10,000 copies earning him an extra £1,000.[3]

His deep evangelical faith and a belief that the Second Coming was imminent, caused much ridicule and obloquy. At the time of the Ten Hours Bill Sydney Smith told Lady Grey that Ashley 'is losing his head and becoming absurd'. Perhaps he will bring forward a Suckling Act – 'No woman to be allowed to suckle her own Children without Medical Certificates.'[4]

His death on 1 October 1885 was followed by widespread expressions of public grief. The funeral was held at Westminster Abbey on 8 October with large crowds present in the streets. He was interred on 9 October in the parish church on his estate at Wimborne St Giles in Dorset.[5]

---

[3] Chadwick, Part 2, pp. 64 – 5.
[4] N. C. Smith (ed.), *Selected Letters of Sydney Smith*, p.225
[5] John Wolffe, 'Cooper, *Anthony Ashley, Seventh Earl of Shaftesbury* (1801–1885)',
ODNB http://www.oxforddnb.com/view/article/6210.

The Earl of Shaftesbury

His memorial in Piccadilly Circus, London, erected in 1893, is crowned by Alfred Gilbert's aluminium statue of Anteros as a nude, winged archer. This is officially titled *The Angel of Christian Charity* but has become popularly, if mistakenly, known as *Eros*. Would Shaftesbury have approved this nude figure on a public monument?

10

Archibald Campbell Tait (1811–82)

Ape's portrait of the Archbishop of Canterbury,
25 December 1869

'An Honest and Liberal Primate'

A Bishop who is at once pious and liberal, who is earnest himself in furtherance of his views, and yet charitable towards those of others, is not so common a product of the times as might be wished; and the pleasure of finding all these qualities in the Primate is therefore all the greater. He is regarded not only with public respect, but also with a personal affection very different from the official regard usually meted out to church dignitaries. He has ever been found to promote the broad and liberal views upon which alone the Church can permanently stand.

Born in Edinburgh to Presbyterian parents, Tait was confirmed into the Church of England whilst at Balliol College, Oxford. He was ordained priest in 1838 and four years later he succeeded Arnold as headmaster of Rugby School, (one of his pupils was Lewis Carroll). He married Catharine Spooner at Rugby in 1843. A serious illness early in 1848, the first of many, which brought him to death's door, made him realise how much the boys loved him despite his remote manner and lack of charisma. He welcomed the comparative leisure that followed upon his appointment to the deanery of Carlisle in 1849. Here he and his wife had to face the most appalling tragedy because in the spring of 1856 within five weeks five of their children died through scarlet fever.

In 1856 Palmerston, advised by Shaftesbury, suggested that Tait, a Broad Churchman, be promoted to London; because of his terrible bereavement the Queen was sympathetic.

Archbishop Longley of Canterbury died at the end of October, 1868, and on the day the Queen heard the news she wrote to Disraeli the Prime Minister suggesting Tait be appointed. 'There is *no* one so fit (indeed the Queen knows of no one who WOULD *be fit* ... he is an excellent, pious, liberal-minded, courageous man'. Disraeli disagreed but fearful of the royal rage backed down, saying to Lord Malmesbury 'don't bring any more bothers before me; I have enough already to drive a man mad'.[1]

Tait was a great supporter of the Establishment of the Church of England and worked with leaders of all parties to strengthen it. He was often in the House of Lords and his robing room was used to lobby peers. Critics have accused him of being responsible for the 1874 Public Worship Regulation Act which attempted to deal with ritualistic clergy, and *Punch* showed him trying to control the ritualistic black sheep with his crook, but it was Shaftesbury and Lord Chancellor Cairns who were responsible for the stricter amendments.[2] Fr Mackonochie was on the point of being deprived of his living when the dying Archbishop saved him by transferring him to another parish.

There was nothing 'churchy' about Tait and he soon became known as 'the layman's Archbishop'. He enjoyed

---

[1] Palmer, *High and Mitred*, p. 75.
[2] Peter Marsh, *Dictionary of National Biography* vol. 53, p. 651.

living in the modern age with its science, railways and new discoveries, and attempted, despite his personal tragedies (in 1878 his wife and only son died) to be an optimist.

He died aged 71 in 1882 and the family were offered burial in Westminster Abbey but declined it. Victoria, to whom he was devoted, asked for a lock of hair, a request she had not even made for Disraeli.

11

Thomas Carlyle (1795–1881)

Ape's cartoon, 22 October 1870

'The Diogenes of the Modern Corinthians without his tub'

For power of word-painting Carlyle has no living equal, and for earnest grasp of the substance beneath the shadow of things no rival in any period. All his characteristics, good or bad, are on a grand scale.

Carlyle belonged to no church so strictly he cannot be described as 'ecclesiastical', but although he left his Calvinism behind when he moved to London his father's theology animated his heart. When his father died he wrote:

> Perhaps my father, all that essentially was my father is even now near me, with me. Both he and I are with God. Perhaps, if it so please God, we shall in some higher state of being meet one another, recognize one another. As it is written, we shall be forever with God.[1]

Carlyle was born in Ecclefechan, Dumfriesshire, the eldest son of a stonemason. He was sent to Annan Academy, six miles away, and in 1809 entered Edinburgh University. Nearly six foot tall he found the rough and tumble of student life difficult, but he excelled in mathematics. His father wanted him to be a minister so he attended

---

[1] Thomas Carlyle, *Reminiscences*, 1:65.

classes in the Divinity Hall, but when he left Edinburgh he had no degree or vocation so became a teacher at his old school.

Returning to Scotland, after a turbulent courtship, he married Jane Welsh on 17 October 1826. Carlyle awakened on his wedding morning in a 'sullen' mood, 'sick with sleeplessness, quite nervous, billus, splenetic and all the rest of it'. Clearly, puritanical inhibitions and romantic idealizations were in the 7 foot-wide bed with two sexual innocents. Fragile evidence suggests that although they were able to express affection with whispers and embraces their sexual relationship did not provide physical satisfaction to either of them, despite their efforts during the first half-dozen or so years of the marriage.[2] Someone later observed that it was just as well they married; otherwise four people would have been desperately unhappy instead of two. It is probable that the marriage was unconsummated.

In 1834 the couple moved to London and settled at Cheyne Row, Chelsea, and he began a book on the French Revolution which occupied him for the next three years. Unfortunately all but four pages of his manuscript was destroyed by a servant who threw it on to the fire thinking it was waste paper. He had to start again, and on 12 January 1837 it was finished; his 'seagreen incorruptible' Robespierre is one of the monsters of literature.[3]

---

[2] Fred Kaplan, 'Carlyle, Thomas (1795–1881)', ODNB
     http://www.oxforddnb.com/view/article/4697
[3] A.N.Wilson, *The Victorians*, p. 17.

On 21 April 1866 Jane had taken her dog to Hyde Park in a brougham but as he jumped from the carriage another carriage hit him. She jumped out to rescue him and collapsed in the brougham with him. She died on the way to hospital, and her husband's sadness and guilt made him more depressed than ever.

Ape's caricature shows a curmudgeon with small leaden eyes, thin body, with slumped shoulders supporting the protruding head on which is the famous wide brimmed straw hat.

'The Sage of Chelsea' was praised by Jehu for his *'grim earnestness and relentless criticism of society'* but in the 1870s Carlyle found little to excite him. 'We are a people drowned in Hypocrisy; saturated with it to the bone – alas ... certain it is, there is nothing but vulgarity in our People's expectations ... it is all a peaceable mouldering or tumbling down from mere rottenness and decay'.[4] As a moralist, in *Past and Present* (1843) he had preached the virtues of work, discipline, thrift and self-help – what today we call Victorian values, but towards the end of his life his hatred of democracy led him to be 'madder and madder, shriller and shriller' as John Kenyon has put it.

On 5 February 1881 he died at home. Four days later the body was conveyed on the overnight train to Scotland and brought to Ecclefechan the next day. The funeral was at noon: as was the custom, the coffin was lowered into the earth without a eulogy or a prayer.[5]

---

[4] *Ibid.* pp.333 – 4.
[5] ODNB.

12

The Revd Alexander Mackonochie (1825–1887)

Ape's caricature, 31 December 1870

'He makes religion a tragedy, and the movements of his muscles a solemn ceremony'

He is one of the latest and most vigorous shoots thrown up by the old Ritualistic stock. He met with the basest insults which he bore with patience.

After a dour and disciplined Scots upbringing he went up to Wadham where he became a disciple of Charles Marriott, a leading Tractarian. Ordained priest in 1850, he was on the staff of Wantage church under William Butler the famous incumbent. Mackonochie's virtues were expressed in a way that made him admirable rather than likeable; he was ascetic, reserved, undemonstrative and heroically stubborn (or perhaps pig-headed). Samuel Wilberforce, his bishop failed to stop him fasting so severely.

In 1856 he joined Charles Lowder to set up a mission in Wapping which later became St Peter, London Docks. Unashamedly ritualistic, the Mission was sure to attract attention and six months later riots began. Some think that it was not ceremonies 'mimicking Popery' or the 'tomfooleries' (Tait) which caused the disturbances, but the way the clergy condemned brothel keepers (there were154 such houses locally) and employers who exploited their work force. Many of the rioters were given money to make trouble. Services were disrupted by boos and catcalls, cushions and hassocks were thrown, and on one occasion 180 constables were unable to maintain order.

On 3 January 1863 he was instituted into the living of St Alban, Holborn. [1] The situation was explosive because the patron and churchwarden, John Hubbard, had no love for ceremonial and had given £55,000 (over £5m today) to build the church. The new vicar agreed not to wear a cassock in the street and give up 'unauthorised novelties and doubtful revivals', and the first five years saw the congregation grow.

The Church Association, founded in 1865 to fight ritualism by litigation, began to take an interest in the parish and two years later persuaded John Martin, a solicitor, to lead the attack. Four successive time-consuming and expensive court cases were brought against Mackonochie on such matters as using lighted candles on the altar, elevation of the chalice and paten at the consecration, the use of incense and mixing water with wine in the chalice. Judgements were sent to Appeal, and as the Association was wealthy proceedings dragged on, and most of the Higher Courts in the land were involved. At one point Mackonochie was suspended for three months so he went on holiday; the Association decide to try to deprive the vicar of his living.

In the autumn of 1882 Tait was on his death bed and, although he had not been a friend of the Tractarians, he felt guilty about such a talented priest being deprived of his living, so his chaplain, Randall Davidson, engineered an exchange of parishes so that Mackonochie went to St

---

[1] His replacement was Fr Ignatius who only lasted for nine months.

Peter, London Docks. A few hours after the formal letter arrived at Addington Palace Tait was dead. One can only marvel at the way Mackonochie had survived the stress of the last few years, but greater unhappiness was to come. In April 1883 the Association pounced, saying that the exchange of livings made no difference and Mackonochie should be inhibited. Lord Penzance, deprived him of his new benefice, and he left at the end of the year.

The next four years were spent in a room at St Alban's clergy house, his health failing. In December 1887 whilst visiting his great friend, the Bishop of Argyll and the Isles, in the Highlands he took the two dogs for a walk and did not return. Search parties went out but it was not until two days later that the body was found with the dogs guarding it. He was only 62.

A huge funeral was held at St Alban, and a long procession walked to Waterloo where a train took the mourners to Brookwood Cemetery in Surrey where the parish has a burial ground.

13

Archbishop Manning (1808–1892)

Ape's caricature of the future Cardinal,
25 February 1871

'The Next Pope'

A man of signal ability and great acquirements. At an age which precludes all explanation of youthful flightiness or folly, he renounced the faith and avowed himself a Roman Catholic. Gifted with the powers that enable men to move their fellows at will by tongue or pen, and blessed with a physical constitution trained to a purely secondary place, he lives an intellectual and spiritual life.

He dines out to talk, but not to eat – he talks to convert, and not to shine; and he is thus become a spare, spiritual, intellectual, elegant, ascetic, whom all respect, whom many fear, and whom none can clearly comprehend. The Church of Rome has duly appreciated and rewarded so distinguished a pervert.

Lytton Strachey in *Eminent Victorians* observed that the Middle Ages lived again in Henry Manning, and Ape's drawing of the stern and ascetic Archbishop is harsh but respectful, placing him in medieval England.

Manning, the son of an MP, was educated at Harrow and Balliol, Oxford, where he was a friend of Gladstone. He was ordained in 1832, and after a curacy at Lavington, Sussex, he became the rector there. In 1833 he married the previous rector's daughter Caroline at a service performed by Samuel Wilberforce, the bride's brother-in-law. Manning's marriage did not last long: his young and beautiful wife came of a consumptive family and she died childless on 24 July 1837.

At the end of 1840 he became Archdeacon of Chichester. The office is usually linked with down-pipes and guttering, but Manning concentrated on the pastoral care of his clergy.

The Revd George Gorham caused much concern to Manning and was probably 'the last straw' which drove him out of the Established Church. Gorham was an Evangelical whose reservations regarding the doctrine of baptismal regeneration had been known since his ordination in 1811. In 1846 he moved to a parish in the Exeter diocese where the Bishop was the choleric High Churchman, Henry Phillpotts. He questioned Gorham for 52 hours and refused to induct and install him. A court case found against Gorham but the Judicial Committee of the Privy Council reversed the decision.

On 6 April 1851, aged 42, Manning was received into the Roman Catholic Church and soon after, on 14 June, was ordained a priest. He knew his move would be deeply unpopular. As Chadwick points out, Wiseman had placed Roman Catholics firmly in English life; Manning wanted them to take their place but felt that his duty lay with the working man. He wrote that after his conversion he felt an alien, exiled, 'like a dead man out of mind'. [1]

Given his great abilities and prior fame, he quickly rose to a position of influence, and, in 1865, was chosen as the second Archbishop of Westminster. He will always be remembered for authorizing the building of

[1] Chadwick part 2 pp 404 – 5.

Westminster Cathedral. When he visited Rome in 1854 Pope Pius IX sent for him; he had met him in 1838 with Gladstone, but since then His Holiness had been forced to flee to Naples until French soldiers brought him back to the Vatican in April 1850. A party of Anglican visitors had not been amused when the Pope greeted them with the blessing usually reserved for incense – 'May thou be blessed by him in whose honour thou shalt be burnt'.

In 1875, Manning was created a Cardinal. He was influential in setting the direction of the modern Roman Catholic Church, and his warm relations with Pope Leo XIII and his ultramontane views gained him the trust of the Vatican. He was among the strongest supporters of the doctrine of papal infallibility.

The Cardinal had a long record of concern for the poor but it was his triumph as a mediator in the Dock Strike of 1889 for which he is best known. His father and brother had been directors of dock companies, but he had close contacts with Ben Tillett the trade union leader. It was to him that the Cardinal went, much to the landlady's surprise. The strike had begun on 14 August, and Manning asked Tillett if he would negotiate.

The next day he sat on a conciliation committee under the Lord Mayor at Mansion House which agreed the increase of sixpence an hour should begin the following March. This was rejected but on 10 September the 81-year-old Archbishop and the MP for Poplar went to meet the strike leaders not in the usual venue (a pub) but in a school. For two hours there was gridlock but then Manning made the last great speech of his life, begging the men to consider their families. By a majority they agreed to Manning's compromise date – 4 November. His triumph was complete and many referred to him as the real Primate of England.[2]

After a few days of illness Manning died on 14 January, 1892. A locket containing his wife's picture was found on a chain around his neck. Thousands paid their respects at his Laying in State in Westminster and later attended his funeral at Kensal Green. His remains were later re-interred in the crypt of his cathedral.

[2] Robert Gray, *Cardinal Manning* (1985), pp. 306 – 311.

14

Alfred Lord Tennyson (1809–1892)

Ape's portrait, 22 July 1871

'The Poet Laureate'

It has become fashionable to doubt his genius and to deprecate his works but he remains unquestionably what the public voice has long pronounced him, the first poet of our day. His songs go straight to the hearts of the most homely. The mere mention of his name awakens in every Englishman an echo of sweet sounds gently rippled into flowing verse. Nevertheless Mr Tennyson is perhaps the poet who has done the most to teach us that there is after all no use in poetry. He lacks the blind driving passion and fierce faith of the very greatest poets. The beautiful and the true seem to act upon him but never to enter into him.

Jehu Junior seems unfair because *The Charge of the Light Brigade*, *The Idylls of the Kings* and *In Memoriam* had already been published and the latter was certainly mystical. It was written to commemorate his dearest friend Arthur Hallam, a poet and fellow student at Trinity College, Cambridge who was engaged to his sister, but died in 1833 from a brain haemorrhage before they could marry. This tragic death forced him to question his faith in God, and to understand his own conflicting feelings about spirituality.

Tennyson was Poet Laureate of the United Kingdom during much of Queen Victoria's reign and remains one of the most popular poets in the English language. When

Albert died he hurried from Freshwater to Osborne, buttoning himself for the occasion into a frock-coat. As he intoned, with his thunderous voice, truths about immortality the Queen thought that his 'rough exterior' went with a 'great mind'.[1]

The son of a clergyman who was a violent drunk and not always sane, Alfred's early poems are not surprisingly dominated by death, despair and loss. Five of his siblings had mental health problems and when he was eleven his father withdrew him from school to educate him at home. In a recent biography John Batchelor points out that the treatment meted out by his grandfather to his father bred in the poet a 'deep social unease', and his difficult childhood laid the foundations for the emotional rawness and sensitivity that characterize his best and most moving poetry.[2]

In 1833 he was appointed Poet Laureate, succeeding William Wordsworth; the night before he dreamt that Prince Albert brought him the letter and kissed him on the cheek – 'very kind but very German'.

Tennyson was not careful with money. In 1842, aged 32, he had sunk the whole of his capital in an invention called the 'Pyroglyph' – a patented system to carve furniture by machine. This was the brain-child of a friend, William Allen who ran a private lunatic asylum. The poet lost every penny, and the family moved to Twickenham. For 19 years after Cambridge he refused employment, staying with friends and going about wearing a floppy-

[1]   Elizabeth Longford, *Victoria R.I.*(1974), p. 342.
[2]   J. Batchelor, *Tennyson* (2012).

brimmed Spanish hat and cloak. Dangling shoulder-length ringlets and a bushy beard completed the outfit.[3]

On 13 June 1850 he married his sister-in-law Emily Sellwood whom he had known since childhood, and they had two children, Hallam and Lionel. As today the Laureate had to churn out poems to mark national occasions and Tennyson dutifully delivered odes for the opening of the Great Exhibition, the marriage of the Prince of Wales, the death of Wellington etc. His wife was much admired and Edward Lear wrote:

> I should think, computing moderately, that 15 angels, several hundreds of ordinary women, many philosophers, a heap of truly wise & kind mothers, 3 or 4 minor prophets, & a lot of doctors and school-mistresses, might all be boiled down, & yet their combined essence fall short of what Emily Tennyson really is. [4]

In 1884 he received a peerage, the first to be given to a poet. Thomas Edison made sound recordings of Tennyson reading his own poetry, which can still be heard. Towards the end of his life Tennyson revealed that his 'religious beliefs also defied convention, leaning towards agnosticism and pandeism'.

Tennyson died on 6 October 1892 at Aldworth, and was buried in Westminster Abbey. A white pall covered

[3] *Ibid.*
[4] V. Noakes, *Edward Lear*, 2nd edn (1979), p. 167.

Alfred Lord Tennyson

his coffin embroidered with the last stanza of his *Crossing the Bar* which today probably makes us wince:

> For tho' from out our bourne of Time and Place
> The flood may bear me far,
> I hope to see my Pilot face to face
> When I have crost the bar.

15

The Revd Charles Voysey (1828–1912)

Coide's cartoon, 21 October 1871

'I have much to be thankful for'

Mr Voysey is a very bold man. A priest of the Church of England, he has stood forth audaciously to preach and to teach in public views which the most hardy even of the laity scarcely dare more than whisper among themselves in private. He declares that the Bible represents the Divinity ... as commanding the destruction of thousands of innocent persons, and as distinguishing with especial favour such men as David, who shamelessly betrayed his friend; Solomon the notorious profligate – Abraham and Isaac, who bartered their wives' virtue for their own safety – and Lot, who invented drunkenness and worse. He refuses to accept the Biblical account of the Divinity as correct. He refuses to believe in the Divinity of Christ.

Voysey was born in London and educated at Stockwell grammar school and St Edmund Hall, Oxford where he graduated in 1851. After ordination he became a curate at Hessle, Yorkshire (1851–58). In 1852 he married Frances Edlin, and they had six daughters and four sons, the eldest being Charles Voysey the architect. He then took an incumbency in Jamaica for two years but returned to Great Yarmouth in 1860, and the following year moved to St Mark, Whitechapel. He was ejected from there for denying the doctrine of eternal punishment. However, he was recommended in 1863 by Bishop Tait of London to the curacy of St Mark, Victoria Docks. Soon he became curate of Healaugh, near Tadcaster, and in 1864 became its vicar, and he remained there for seven years. In that year he published a sermon *Is Every Statement in the Bible about our Heavenly Father Strictly True?* This was withdrawn, but he then began to publish his sermons under the title *The Sling and the Stone*, which continued for six years and over 1,250,000 copies were sold.

In 1871 Voysey appeared before the Chancellor of York and was deprived of his living because he denied original sin, asserted that justification by faith is contrary to Christ's teaching and held that large numbers of New Testament passages were spurious. He appealed to the Judicial Committee of the Privy Council but they in 1871 upheld the decision.

Having lost his benefice and income he moved to London and began to hold services in St George's Hall, Langham Place, and then founded the 'Theistic Church' which met in Swallow Street, off Regent Street. Services were very similar to Anglican ones and over the next 30 years they attracted large congregations.

Voysey's ultimate theological position amounted to the rejection of the creeds, biblical inspiration, the sacramental system, and the divinity of Christ, and his teaching was the inculcation of a pure theism, without any miraculous element. He was an attractive preacher, courageous and sincere; one of his congregation was Annie Besant. He was a founder member of the Cremation Society of England so when he died aged 84 at his home in Hampstead, his body was cremated at Golders Green on 24 July 1912.

16

Charles Kingsley 1819–1875

Adriano Cecioni's caricature, 30 March 1872

'The Apostle of the Flesh'

Anglican priest, university professor, historian and novelist, he was born in Devon. He epitomised Muscular Christianity because he was a born athlete and thought that games were conducive to physical and moral health.

He was one of the most daring and advanced revolutionists of the cloth. The Socialistic agitations and aspirations were at their height when he commenced his career and he wrote and preached with ardent sympathy for the cause of the labouring and oppressed.

Kingsley was deeply involved in the religious, scientific and social conflicts of his time and was one of the first to praise Darwin's *The Origin of Species* although some ridiculed his campaigns on behalf of cold water, pure air and physical exercise. He himself suffered from a stutter and admitted to his wife Fanny, who he married in 1844, that he had periods of black despair. In his letters to her he is revealed as a man of strong sensuous passions and frustrations.[1] It was as the writer of *The Water Babies*, a fairy tale about a boy chimney sweep, that he achieved fame.

After studying at King's College, London Kingsley moved to Magdalene, Cambridge. Lonely, intensely shy,

[1] See Susan Chitty, *The Beast and the Monk* (1974).

and physically restless, he gradually found companionship through rowing and riding to hounds, and graduated in 1842. His first living was at Eversley in Hampshire, and he was profoundly influenced by the social unrest of the 'Hungry Forties'. When the Chartist movement organized a major demonstration at Kennington Common in 1848 he was there as a supporter, and with his friend F. D. Maurice he threw himself into a controversial new Christian socialist movement devoted to spreading this gospel and to setting up co-operative workshops for tailors and other oppressed trades. That year, on Maurice's recommendation, Kingsley obtained a part-time appointment as professor of English at the newly-formed Queen's College for Women in London, but he was briefly banned from preaching in the diocese of London. [2] Over the next decade he published several historical novels such as *Westward Ho!*

On Palm Sunday 1859 Kingsley preached for the first time at Buckingham Palace clutching a thousand word sermon in accordance with the royal command. Victoria liked his simplicity and directness, and made him there and then a Chaplain in Ordinary.

In 1860, on the recommendation of Prince Albert he became Regius Professor of Modern History at Cambridge, moving to be a canon of Chester in 1870. Three years later he, at Gladstone's invitation, moved to be a canon of Westminster. The Prime Minister wrote

[2] Norman Vance, 'Kingsley, Charles (1819–1875)', *Oxford Dictionary of National Biography*,http://www.oxforddnb.com/view/article/15617.

that he was sorry 'to injure the people of Chester; but I must sincerely hope your voice will be heard within the Abbey, and in your own right'. Sadly he was to stay less than two years before he died on 23 January 1875 aged 56, and was buried in Eversley churchyard.

Dean Stanley in an Abbey sermon after Kingsley's death rightly picked upon the one consistent feature in a seemingly inconsistent character, the endless striving to improve the lot of the poor.

17

The Revd Dr Charles Vaughan (1816–1897)

Montbard's cartoon, 24 August 1872

'Nolo Episcopari'

Harrow was nowhere on the list of great schools when he became its Head. At Doncaster he made a sensible and manly protest against the annual vote of £2,000 made by the Town Council for the promotion of gambling. They took no notice.

He is a chaplain to the Queen, an office which confers more glory than gain, the stipend being only £30 a year.[1] He is a preacher of the most eloquent and persuasive order, gentle, earnest, scholarly, tolerant.

Vaughan entered Trinity College Cambridge in 1834 and became a Fellow five years later before leaving to be vicar of St Martin Leicester. He became Headmaster of Harrow in 1845 and found the school in disarray. There were 69 boys living in substandard conditions – there was no bathtub between them. During the next 15 years, Vaughan, who had studied under Dr Arnold at Rugby, transformed the school and at one point there were 488 pupils.

Following Arnold he provided a religious and moral education and as a reward he became a wealthy man. Everyone expected he would be given a mitre but suddenly and unexpectedly he left Harrow in 1859 to become vicar of Doncaster. What no one knew at the

[1] Approximately £2,700 in 2011.

time was that he had had a homosexual affair with Alfred Pretor, one of his Upper Sixth, who told a fellow student, John Addington Symonds who told his father. John himself had been propositioned numerous times, and a master at Harrow had already intercepted a note between two of the boys, and passed it to Vaughan who summoned the whole school immediately, and read the letter aloud. He then flogged both culprits.

Symonds' father threatened him with exposure, so he resigned and shortly afterwards had to refuse the bishopric of Rochester. His wife, the sister of Arthur Stanley later Dean of Westminster, went to see Symonds and on her knees asked him to have mercy but he refused.[2] Tyerman's history of the school[3] suggests that the story is true and he has unearthed some corroborating evidence – including a steamy letter to another young favourite, apparently written while he was invigilating a school exam. His sermonizing masked a brutish commitment to flogging (he insisted on a new birch each time and liked to leave the birch buds painfully embedded in the wounds) and did little to change the behaviour of the boys: Vaughan's Harrow appears to have been dominated by bullying, drinking and fighting. The cleverest boys, not to mention the masters, saw through him as a shallow, ignorant, literal-minded man, who (as Tyerman puts it) 'compensated for his small mind with expansive care for his pupils'. However John Roach in the 2004 DNB

---

[2]   Palmer, *High and Mitred*, p. 55.
[3]   Christopher Tyerman, *A History of Harrow School* (2000).

says the story of the affair is 'not proven',[4] and a new biography (2013) by Trevor Park refutes the story.

At Doncaster he trained men for the ministry; his 'doves' as he called them. By the end of his life there were 450 of them. One was the 23-year-old Randall Davidson who went to Vaughan at the Temple and began a course of reading. Davidson wrote:

> Vaughan had an extraordinary power of bringing out from the text of scripture things new and old. We wrote sermons for him every week. He would not object unless it were with placid humour and wit, to our putting forth opinions of an ecclesiastical sort with which he had little or no sympathy.[5]

In 1869 he had been appointed Master of the Temple and this time Symonds raised no objection. By 1879 when he became Dean of Llandaff Symonds was dead. The story did not come to light until the 1960s.

Vaughan maintained his friendship with Alfred Pretor until his death and at his request he undertook the duties of his literary executor. He died in 1897 in the Llandaff deanery and was buried within the cathedral grounds.

[4] DNB vol. 56, J. Roach, pp. 160 – 162.
[5] G.K.A.Bell, *Randall Davidson* vol 1, p. 27f.

18

Arthur Penhryn Stanley (1815–1881)

Montbard's drawing of the Dean of Westminster,
21 September 1872

'Philosophic Belief'

As a student at Oxford he was endowed with above average intellectual powers and of a supple and trimming character. Now 58 he became Dean of Westminster in 1864. He is one of the great ornaments of the church, and is a favourite in society and makes tea upon occasions for the highest Personage in the Realm. He has a good presence and a clear voice. His sermons leave a lasting impression.

Stanley was born in Alderley Edge in Cheshire, where his father, who later became Bishop of Norwich, was rector. At Rugby School under Dr Arnold he probably acquired his air of honesty and manliness, and he is generally considered to be the source for the character of George Arthur in Thomas Hughes's book *Tom Brown's Schooldays*. In 1834 he went up to Balliol College, Oxford and five years later was elected a Fellow of University College; in the same year he took holy orders. After a spell as a canon of Canterbury he was appointed Regius professor of ecclesiastical history at Oxford in 1856, a post which, with the attached canonry at Christ Church, he held for seven years.

In 1863 Queen Victoria was not amused. Lady Augusta Bruce, one of her Household and a close confidante, had at the age of 41 decided to marry a 48-year-old clergyman – Arthur Stanley, who had just been appointed Dean of Westminster. 'She has most unnecessarily decided to marry (!!!)', the Queen selfishly told King Leopold, 'It has been my greatest sorrow and trial since my misfortune'. Her Ladyship persevered, but Stanley in a letter to his bride said that he had doubts about the wisdom of leaving Oxford 'for that Church of Tombs', and these fears were made worse when he met the canons. One of them, Christopher Wordsworth, had already preached against the appointment which elicited a lunch invitation from the new Dean who still remained gloomy. However, over the next 17 years he became one of the most distinguished deans in the Abbey's 900 year history, and within four years he had written his scholarly, encyclopaedic *Historical Memorials of Westminster Abbey*.[1]

The Dean, who had already published eleven major books including a Life of Dr Arnold, acknowledged that he had little interest in church music but his gifts meant that he set out to make the Abbey the centre of religious and national life in a truly liberal spirit. He wanted it to be the visual embodiment of the national Church. However, he did not allow the first Lambeth Conference (1867) to worship in the Abbey, saying that the bishops had not been summoned by a secular authority.

This lovable man was totally impractical and lived on buttered toast; He could not peel a boiled egg, his wife did it for him. He wore ordinary clerical dress because he did not know how to button his gaiters.[2]

---

[1] Malcolm Johnson, *Crypts of London* (2013).
[2] A. N. Wilson reviewing *Excellent Dr Stanley* by John Witheridge in TLS, 8 Nov 2013.

Stanley took a very close interest in the excavations beneath the Abbey floor. Workmen found the coffins of Charles II, Mary II, William III, Prince George of Denmark and Queen Anne with urns at the feet. But where was James 1? Stanley and his researchers were baffled, and agreed they should now look beneath the tomb of Elizabeth I. By now the Chapel must have resembled a building site. Then a narrow vault was discovered containing the anthropoid lead coffins of Henry VII, Elizabeth his Queen and James I; all were in good condition.[3]

Stanley invited men of all shades of opinion to preach, began 'special services' in the nave and arranged for a performance of Bach's St Matthew Passion in 1871. The building was opened more to the public although protection had to be taken, as today, against 'mischievous boys, eccentric or crazy persons, and relic hunters'. Prothero's readable biography describes a dream in which Stanley was elected Pope but had to discuss with Athenaeum members what name to take.

Victoria liked broad churchmen and her ideal clergyman was Stanley, who was broadest of the broad,[4] indeed he coined the phrase 'Broad Church', saying in 1850 that the Church of England was a latitudinarian body which included 'opposite and contradictory opinions'. That is its strength.

Victoria called him 'the little Dean' (he was only 5ft 5 ¼ inches tall). However she did find him 'of no sex' and

[3] For a full account see M.A. Johnson, *Crypts of London*, 2013, pp. 80 – 83.
[4] Chadwick Part 2, p. 339.

'cold' compared to the tender-hearted Dean Wellesley. Stanley died in 1881 and was buried in Henry VII's Chapel, in the same grave as his wife who had died in 1876, and whose death left him desolate.

19

Anthony Trollope (1815–1882)

Spy cartoon of the novelist, 5 April 1873

'A Novelist'

Mr Trollope is a student and delineator of costume rather than humanity. He does not, as George Eliot does, pry into the great problems of life, or attempt to show the mournful irony of fate. He is not a deep thinker, but he is an acute observer, and with the knack of divining what most impresses the commonplace people who most delight in novels. He is a correct painter of the small things of our small modern English life so far as it presents itself to the eye – deeper than this he does not go. Good natured and genial as becomes a successful man, his manners are a little rough, as is his voice. For many years he has amused readers without ever shocking them.

Jehu Junior obviously did not care for Trollope. Usually he snipes, but here heavy artillery is used. He would be surprised that his novels are still popular and some have been filmed. Spy's cartoon is also less than flattering, with the thumb held erect whilst smoking and his coat buttoned once and then parting over a small but comfortable corporation. Whilst walking with the novelist on St George's Hill near Walton, Ward tells us that Trollope 'admired the scenery and I noted the beauties of Nature in another way committing those mental reservations to my mental notebook, and came home to what fun I could get out of them'. When the caricature appeared,

Trollope was furious and Ward received a 'stiff letter' from his publisher who had introduced him.[1]

Money, or rather the lack of it, played a large part in Trollope's early life although he did attend Harrow and Winchester. In 1834 aged 19, he received an offer of a clerkship in the General Post Office but he acquired a reputation for unpunctuality and insubordination. A debt of £12 to a tailor fell into the hands of a moneylender and grew to over £200; the lender regularly visited him at his office to demand payments. Trollope hated his work, but saw no alternatives and lived in constant fear of dismissal.

Fortunately he was able to secure a job as a postal surveyor's clerk in central Ireland. His salary and travel allowance went much farther in Ireland than they had in London, and he found himself enjoying a measure of prosperity. In 1844 he married Rose Heseltine, the daughter of a Rotherham bank manager.

Trollope began writing on the numerous long train trips around Ireland he had to take to carry out his postal duties. Setting very firm goals about how much he would write each day, he eventually became one of the most prolific writers of all time. In 1851, Trollope was sent to England, charged with investigating and reorganizing rural mail delivery in a portion of the country. The two-year mission took him over much of Great Britain, often on horseback. And when he visited Salisbury Cathedral he conceived the plot of *The Warden*.

In 1859, he obtained a position in the Post Office as Surveyor to the Eastern District, and moved to Waltham

[1]   Leslie Ward, *Forty Years of Spy*, p.104 – 5.

Cross. In 1867, he resigned his position at the Post Office, and concentrated solely on his writing.

Trollope is first and foremost a novelist who thrives on characterization. His cast of characters places clergy in their natural habitat from the bishop (and Mrs Proudie) in the Palace to Mr Quiverful in his hamlet. His stories were often close to reality.

He increasingly moved towards the kind of liberalism in religion that Newman and Keble so hated. His acceptance of the Church of England as a comfortably irrational institution is reflected in his novels and their characters, such as Mrs Proudie, Mr Slope and Archdeacon Grantley.

Anthony did not believe in the literal resurrection of the body; in 1874, eight years before his death, he was, with Millais, one of the sixteen founders of the Cremation Society. It was to be another ten years before cremation was legalised so he was buried at Kensal Green.

20

The Revd Edward Bouverie Pusey (1800–1882)

Ape's caricature, 2 January 1875

'High Church'

50 years ago he was a boy of marvellous precocity, an infant prodigy but not content with taking the highest honours and gliding through them down a gentle incline of dead languages and ecclesiastical preferment, he became a student at a German University known for attacks on the orthodox Evangelical Faith of the Anglican Church. From Germany he brought back not only the fatal spirit of reason but also a knowledge of Hebrew. Aged 28 he became Regius Professor at Oxford and was the most prominent apostle of the Tractarian Movement.

Never dining out he passes his time in an inaccessible study in company with a crucifix and entrenched behind the heaviest works that theology has produced. Shy beyond conception and hating ostentation of all kind, he works on University committees ... and allows himself no other recreation than that of confessing nuns. The most astounding fact about Dr Pusey is that he did marry.

Ape portrays the 75 year old in his declining years, his doleful countenance and heavy eyes look back upon a lifetime of sadness, struggles and controversies. There is an undercurrent of pessimism and gloom probably caused by the death of his wife Maria after only 11 years of married life in 1839; he always looked down when crossing Tom Quad because he could still see the white pall on Maria's coffin fluttering in the wind at the funeral. Newman arrived within the hour to comfort him – 'it was like the visit of an angel'. Three of his four children died before him so he became a recluse, until Keble talked him out of it.[1]

He was born in the village of Pusey in Berkshire, his father being a younger son of Viscount Folkestone. After Eton (under 'Flogger' Keate)[2] and Christchurch he was elected to a fellowship at Oriel College where his friends included Newman and Keble. Conscious of the disturbing developments in German biblical scholarship and theology, Pusey learnt German, Hebrew and Arabic.

In 1828 he was ordained and made Regius Professor of Hebrew by Gladstone. Pusey occupied the chair of theology for over fifty years and after 1835 joined the Oxford Movement when he published Tracts on baptism and fasting, then began the *Library of the Fathers*. More controversial was a sermon he preached eight years later on the Eucharist. Using an ancient law the authorities suspended him for two years from preaching, with the result that 18,000 copies of the sermon were sold.

Pusey, Newman and Keble were the leaders of the Tractarians so he was deeply upset by Newman's secession. They did not meet for 19 years, then by chance they were both at Keble's house in 1865 so dined together for the last time.

[1] Leonard Prestige, *Pusey* (Mowbray 1981), pp. 44 – 59.
[2] Revd Dr John Keate, Headmaster of Eton 1809–34, was a stocky 5-footer with flaming red hair. Brutal and sadistic, on one occasion he birched 80 boys in one morning.

Not many Regius Professors spend the Long Vacation tending cholera victims in Bethnal Green, but that is what Pusey did in 1867. He died on 16 September 1882, after a short illness, and was buried at Oxford in the cathedral of which he had been for fifty-four years a canon. In his memory his friends purchased his library, and bought for it a house in Oxford, known as the Pusey House, opened in 1884.

21

The Revd Charles Old Goodford DD (1812–84)

Spy's cartoon, 22 January 1876

'Old Goody'

*At Eton he was a respected and popular assistant master,
a trifle pompous but firm, not a transcendent. He was
appointed Provost in 1862. Now he is 64.He did little to
increase the learning of Etonians, for his only achievement
in this way was to add mathematics to the compulsory
curriculum of studies; but he bore himself right worthily in
his silk cassock. He was not a fit aspirant to the Episcopal
Bench, for St Paul has said that a bishop should be 'no
striker' and such a description hardly applies to one who
has flourished the birch over half the future Peerage.*

*A thoroughly good man ... he is yet simple, plain and
unpretending ... he has turned out some of the best men that
in modern times have left Eton ... without making prigs of
them.*

Educated at Eton and King's College, Cambridge he
received his doctorate in 1853. He returned to Eton and
became an assistant-master then a house-master. On 28
March 1844 he married Katharine Lucia and thus had
to forfeit his Fellowship at King's. He was a liberal and
kind housemaster, but his management was not equal
to his good intentions. In 1853 he became Head Master
with the responsibility for the day-to-day management of
the school. He restructured the teaching and discipline
but would have done more if the Provost (Chairman of

the governors) had agreed. In 1862 he himself became Provost – rather unwillingly as his salary was cut.

Spy had been a small boy in the school under Goodford's headship, and later considered his portrait of him 'one of my best early caricatures'. He stalked him in Eton High Street, but Goodford protested that he never carried an umbrella in this way. However, he later saw his reflection in a shop window and with astonishment told his wife 'Spy was right after all'.[1]

Great changes and improvements were made in the college under Goodford's leadership, and he remained at Eton until his death at The Lodge, Eton College, on 9 May 1884. He was buried in the Eton cemetery on 14 May.

[1]   Leslie Ward, *Forty Years*, pp.223 – 4.

22

The Hon and Very Revd Gerald Valerian Wellesley (1809–1882)

Spy's cartoon, 8 April 1876

'The Old Dean'

The old Dean has refrained from the high theological questions of his time, he has not ventured into literature. He and his wife have had the honour of nursing the religious and of directing the ecclesiastical patronage of Her Majesty the Queen. He is a gentlemanly man of mild opinions and of no particular heresy...beyond being a martyr to his liver.

A nephew of the Iron Duke, Wellesley went to Eton and Trinity College, Cambridge, where he was a contemporary of Gladstone. He was ordained in 1831 and was incumbent of the family living of Stratfield Saye from 1836 to 1854. On 16 September 1856 he married the Hon. Magdalen 'Lily' Montagu and they had one son, who died at the age of eighteen in 1883. Aged 40 he was made Domestic Chaplain to the Queen.

Spy followed the Dean on one of his early morning walks outside the Round Tower. Wellesley was not pleased at the result, particularly because his wife told him 'You have had that hat for 25 years; get rid of it'.

He refused Aberdeen's offer of the bishopric of Bath and Wells in1854, but aged 45 accepted the Deanery of Windsor so became someone who the Queen and Prime Minister consulted on appointments. Two years later he sent a memorandum to Prince Albert pointing out that bishops were chosen for their political party instead of their church party which led to 'very inferior specimens, safe men'.

Wellesley was at the Prince Consort's deathbed standing opposite Victoria on 14 December 1861, and after Albert had died the Queen was carried into the next room. 'We heard her loud sobs' he told his brother. The Queen appreciated his ministry and when five years later the Princess Royal's son died said the best kind of comforter was the 'tender hearted' Wellesley. A preacher of short sermons, he became one of Victoria's most valued advisers.[1] Concerned that her relationship with John Brown was helping assuage her grief she consulted the Dean who reassured her that God sometimes placed sympathetic people in the path of those who mourn; they provide comfort and consolation.[2]

The Dean had definite views. When Canterbury was vacant in 1868 one candidate was the Bishop of Gloucester who Wellesley told the Queen 'has a miserably thin, weak voice, and no dignity of manner ... an amiable, insignificant man, talking constantly and irrelevantly.' He was not appointed. When he died in September 1882 and was buried in St George's Windsor, Victoria began to look for a successor to 'the most charming of all ecclesiastical berths'. She wanted

'A tolerant liberal-minded, Broad Church clergyman who at the same time is pleasant socially and is

---

[1] *Beloved Mama: Private Correspondence of Queen Victoria and the German Crown Princess, 1878–1885*, ed. R. Fulford (1981), p. 125.
[2] C. Hibbert, *Queen Victoria* (2000), p. 328.

popular with all members and classes...a good, kind man without pride.'

In other words, another Wellesley.

23

Henry Parry Liddon (1829–1890)

Spy's cartoon, 16 September 1876

'High Church'

Dr Liddon is a rhetorician with notions. He left Cuddesdon in consequence of having developed views higher in the Church sense than the Bishop cared to countenance. He has succeeded to Dr Pusey's position as the recognized Leader of High Church at Oxford. Gladstone has always liked Liddon so made room for him at St Paul's Cathedral. A master of the English language but it is rather in speaking than in writing it. As a preacher to cultivated theologians he has indeed no equal, and of that kind the men admire him to the verge of conviction, the women beyond the verge of adoration. His manners are excellent; his sermons are long and monotonous though sometimes relieved by biting sarcasm.

The son of a naval captain, Liddon was educated at Christ Church Oxford where he was appointed to a Studentship which he was to hold for life. In 1854 he became Vice Principal of Cuddesdon theological College near Oxford; one wag said that the college was known for its vices not its principles. In 1870 he was made canon of St Paul's Cathedral where his preaching attracted large crowds. The Sunday afternoon sermon, had usually been delivered in the choir, but soon after his appointment it was moved to under the dome, where between 3,000 to 4,000 persons gathered to hear him.

At Oxford one of Liddon's closest friends was Lewis Carroll, three years older, and they often rowed on the river together, where Carroll took one of the most famous photographs of his friend. In 1867 they visited Russia together and had 'long arguments' usually about religion; unlike Liddon, Carroll disliked the Roman Catholic Church.

Spooner wrote that listening to a Liddon sermon was an 'intellectual treat'. Sermons could be an hour long but his clear, thrilling, penetrating voice, the admirable order and lucidity of his discourse, its clear-cut outlines and incisiveness, its picturesque vividness of detail, the exhaustiveness with which the topic was treated, its argumentative power, the flashes of lambent sarcasm with which the argument was lit up, combined to make a perfect whole which it was a delight to listen to. Yet perhaps as a preacher he suffered from two defects; he was too often combative, and could be sarcastic. [1]

He and Dean Church and Canon Gregory were able to move the Cathedral worship in a Tractarian direction, and when the Purchas Judgement of 1871 ruled that the eastward position of the celebrant at communion was illegal, Gregory and Liddon told the Bishop of London that they had no intention of complying. They were summoned to see Bishop Jackson, who told them he would only act if the authorities at the cathedral desired it.[2] Liddon loathed legislation that bullied the clergy and visited Fr Tooth in prison.

---

[1] W. Hayter, *Spooner*, p. 153.
[2] Keene, Burns and Saint (eds.), *St Paul's* (2004), p. 357.

In 1885 Gladstone wanted Liddon to be a bishop, but the Queen disliked Tractarians and nothing came of it. Three years later his name was mentioned for Oxford but Victoria thought that he might 'ruin and taint' the undergraduates as his closest friend Pusey had done. Lord Salisbury did offer him St Albans, but he refused, and was dead six months later, aged only 61. He is buried in St Paul's.

24

John Henry Newman (1801–1890)

Spy's cartoon of the future Cardinal,
20 January 1877

'Tracts for the Times'

One of the greatest intellectual theologians England has ever produced and one of the least rewarded. In Tract Ninety he blew a blast which shook the whole fabric of the Church to its very foundations. His secession came upon the Anglican Church as a crushing blow, under which, as Mr Disraeli said, it reeled and from which it has not yet recovered and never will.

But there was still no rest and no acceptance for this profound thinker and marvellous writer. The Roman Church at once felt that in him it had gained a white elephant, rare and valuable indeed beyond all price, but most expensive to keep. He declared the dogma of Infallibility as 'a lie forced on the Church by an insolent and aggressive faction'. He has had far more affliction and sorrow to bear in the Church of his adoption than in that of his birth.

Newman, born in 1801, went up to Trinity College Oxford in 1817 then became a tutor at Oriel until he was appointed vicar of St Mary's the university church in1828. He stayed 15 years and his sermons profoundly influenced the new Oxford Movement which he helped to launch. His Tract 90 (1841) created a storm of protest by asserting that the Thirty-Nine Articles of the Anglican Church were Catholic in spirit and intent. The following year Bishop Bagot of Oxford said that the

Tracts were beneficial, but Tract XC was objectionable and regrettable because it made the 39 Articles mean anything or nothing.

In 1842 whilst still at St Mary's he made his home at Littlemore and was joined by several young men including Ambrose St John, aged 28, who was to fill the emotional gap in Newman's life caused by the death of Hurrell Froude. Was a monastery being founded? Definitely not, he told the Bishop; his 'cloisters' were a shed connecting the converted stables. Half-way through his life, on 9 October 1845 he was received into the Roman Catholic Church. The following year he went to Rome, where he was ordained priest. At the close of 1847, Newman returned to England as an Oratorian, finally settling at Edgbaston where (except for four years in Ireland) he lived a secluded life for nearly forty years. Before moving to Edgbaston he had established the London Oratory.

Newman was also a literary figure of note: his major writings including his autobiography *Apologia Pro Vita Sua* (1865–66), and the poem *The Dream of Gerontius* (1865), which was set to music in 1900 by Edward Elgar as an oratorio and contains the hymn 'Praise to the Holiest in the Height'.

The offer of a cardinal's hat was made in February 1879. He remained in Birmingham and Ward was on his way to 'stalk' Newman when he saw him at Euston Station so followed him into the buffet and watched him drinking his soup, but this was not good enough so a few days later he went to Birmingham and asked a priest what time the Cardinal would be going out. The man thought he wanted an interview so went to arrange it, but Spy bolted. His caricature accentuated Newman's large nose, small mouth, slight figure and drooping shoulders.

On 11 August 1890 he died of pneumonia at the Birmingham Oratory. Eight days later, his body was buried in the cemetery at Rednal Hill, Birmingham, at the country house of the Oratory. In accordance with his express wishes, Newman was buried in the grave of his lifelong friend, Ambrose St John. Their relationship has been much discussed in recent years, but it seems likely that they were celibate homosexuals. His grave was opened on 2 October 2008, but his wooden coffin was found to have disintegrated and no bones were found.

Newman's beatification was officially proclaimed by Pope Benedict XVI on 19 September 2010 during his visit to the United Kingdom.

25

The Revd Arthur Tooth (1839–1931)

Spy's cartoon, 10 February 1877

'The Christian Martyr'

Now 38 he is a quiet, amiable unaggressive priest. At Hatcham he became one of those who affirm by the ritual and ceremonies they use the continuity of the Catholic Succession in the Anglican Church. Much howling and adverse pressure, physical as well as moral, became habitual at Hatcham. Lord Penzance fulminated a judgement which Mr Tooth disobeyed and was thereupon sent to prison where he remains a glory to his friends and a gigantic difficulty to his foes.

He is an ascetic, devoted, earnest, honest man incapable of seeing two sides to any question ... endowed less with a great power of will than with an enormous power of won't.

Ward wanted to sketch Tooth, but how could he get into Holloway Gaol? Bowles, the proprietor, thought about it then said 'I'm the Secretary to the Persian Relief Fund'. This seemed irrelevant but much to his surprise Ward was able to observe 'the Reverend gentleman as he posed behind the bars'.[1]

After Tonbridge School and Trinity College Cambridge and three short curacies, Tooth had been inducted at St James Hatcham in 1868. A typical South London suburb it had a population of 10,000. The church was run-down and the fabric was infested with 'moths, spiders, black

---

[1] Ward, *Forty Years of Spy*, p. 133.

beetles ... whose time of excommunication had come'. Young and slim, he looked elegant in clericals - 'priestly rather than manly'. A first step was to abolish pew rents so that the poor would be encouraged to worship. Tooth set up 14 organisations which provided various activities and his school provided servers and choir.[2]

In 1874 three members of the Church Association, who were not parishioners, began proceedings to stop the use of vestments, incense, altar lights, etc. In all there were 18 charges. The case came before Lord Penzance in the Court of Arches at Lambeth Palace on 13 July 1876 but Tooth refused to acknowledge the Court's jurisdiction. Penzance inhibited the vicar from taking services for three months. The Bishop sent a priest to officiate but he was not granted access. On the Sunday after Christmas the riots began, and the numbers involved were huge. The Association paid men to disrupt the services and on 5 January 1877 there were between 5,000 and 8,000 outside the building; the police on duty took no action.

The press enjoyed it all, as did some churchmen. The Bishop of Peterborough, William Magee, commented 'The extraction of Tooth goes on. I wish the Church could be chloroformed; out he must come'. On the 22nd the vicar was arrested and taken to the debtors' wing of the Horsemonger Lane Gaol at the south end of London Bridge, but he was allowed to leave on 17 February and left for the continent to rest and recover. Now 39, he resigned and never worked as a parish priest again. It is

---

[2] B. Palmer, *Reverend Rebels* (1993), p. 119.

ironic that shortly afterwards the sentence against him was declared null and void on a technicality.

Thanks to a legacy of £10,000 (approx £928,000 today) Tooth now purchased a house near Croydon where he was able to run a school for orphan boys, a sisterhood and a home for alcoholics. He died on 5 March 1931.

26

The Earl of Beaconsfield (1804–1881)

Ape's caricature of Disraeli, 2 July 1878

'The Junior Ambassador'

Jehu Junior detested Gladstone but greatly admired Disraeli, who he portrayed three times. Above he is captured in the House, with a languid pose, doleful look, drooping lower lip, an air of insouciance, eyes half-closed, lapsing into simulated sleep.

Baptised in Holborn through the careful foresight of his father the boy became the first titular Christian of his family; and he had scarcely left school when finding the world before him, and in himself a great contempt for it, he formed the resolution to be Somebody. He had all the qualities that command success – a great contempt for the dull English, among whom as though by providential dispensation, his life had fallen, wonderful talents, a grand confidence in himself, and no prejudices.

The son of a 'privileged race', for which he was despised, scarcely admitted to be an Englishman, poor, landless, in debt and in difficulties, the squires and families who then ruled in England looked upon him as an incredible joke, probably invented by a sympathetic Providence for their after-dinner pastime ... His maiden speech, delivered on 7th December 1837, was contemptuously hooted down.

Personally he is most charming, sympathetic and playful. In ladies he delights and behaves to them always like a gentleman ... As a speaker there is no man makes a greater effect ... he always displays audacity, but he lacks courage and despises constancy.

Benjamin Disraeli was born in London, the second of five children of Isaac and Maria D'Israeli. He attended private schools then was baptised as an Anglican on 31 July 1817 so went to Higham Hill School, Epping. In November 1821 he was articled for three years at a solicitors firm but he decided not to be a lawyer; he dreamed instead of literary fame. From the early 1820s he had adopted an appropriately eye-catching and narcissistic style of dress, with ruffled shirts, velvet trousers, coloured waistcoats, and jewellery, and he wore his hair in cascades of ringlets. Financial disaster now made him moody and depressed, but in 1837 he became MP for Maidstone

Having always been attracted by older women he married a wealthy widow, Mary Anne, on 28 August 1839, and she paid off his huge debts. Ten years later his father and brother enabled them to buy the small country house of Hughenden Manor, outside High Wycombe. It became a status symbol but he neither shot nor hunted and disliked country-house visiting with its conventions, its 'constant dressing & indigestion' and its masculine conversations. [1]

In the 1852 government he was made Chancellor of the Exchequer. When he expressed his financial ignorance Derby, the PM, told him, 'They give you the figures'. Before and during his political career, Disraeli was well

---

[1] Jonathan Parry, *Disraeli, Benjamin, Earl of Beaconsfield (1804–1881)*, ODNB http://www.oxforddnb.com/view/article/7689

known as a literary and social figure. He mainly wrote romances, of which *Sybil* and *Vivian Grey* are perhaps the best-known today.

Dizzy became Prime Minister in 1868, then again in1874. He commented that 'Nothing gives me more trouble than the Episcopacy. There are so many parties, so many schools of thought in the Church'. Despite worshipping regularly at Hughenden, he had never moved in ecclesiastical circles so was ignorant of the men needing preferment and thought high-church ritualists were a 'finical and fastidious crew' who were 'as corrosively subversive of church power as the radical dissenters'.[2]

Disraeli became the Earl of Beaconsfield, and a recent biography[3] suggests that he saw politics as a game with no moral content. Progressive policies such as slum improvement, public health measures and a new Factory Act were driven by his Home Secretary, Richard Cross. Dizzy preferred the international stage, and spent considerable sums on wars in South Africa and Afghanistan. Dominic Sandbrook points out that there have been few cinematic Gladstones but plenty of Disraeli. 'It is such a showy part – half Satan, half Don Juan, he could write novels, flatter a Queen, dig the Suez Canal. Present her with India. You can't beat that, it's better than Wyatt Earp'.[4]

---

[2]   ODNB.
[3]   Douglas Hurd and Edward Young, *Disraeli Or, the Two Lives* (2013).
[4]   Dominic Sandbrook, *The Sunday Times*, 7.7.2013.

On his deathbed Disraeli declined a visit from his Queen – 'She will only ask me to take a message to Albert'.[5] He died in April 1881 and is buried in a churchyard vault near his home at Hughenden Manor.

[5] Palmer, p.83.

27

Lieut-Col Charles Gordon (1833–85)

Ape's caricature, 19 February 1881

'The Ever Victorious'

The most notable of living Englishmen. He comes of a soldier race. At the Military Academy he remained for five years, a hopeless 'pickle' who once received a special rebuke and reduction to the ranks from Lord Anglesey. In China he was wounded once, and had the most marvellous escapes, yet he never went armed himself with more than a bamboo stick.

Colonel Gordon, who had been travelling and triangulating about the Great Wall, was put at the head of the force and became 'Chinese Gordon'. He reorganised the force, which had always been and always continued to be prone to disorder and mutiny. They fought over 30 desperate battles and finally reconquered China with his three thousand men for the Manchoo dynasty.

This disappointing cartoon was drawn three years before the Siege of Khartoum which was to ensure Gordon's name a place in the British Pantheon. However, he had already made a name for himself in China, so Pellegrini could have drawn him in his robes.

Gordon was born in Woolwich to a military family, and after school in Taunton he entered the Royal Military Academy, Woolwich, and in 1852 he was commissioned in the Royal Engineers. He served in the Crimea with conspicuous gallantry, but made his reputation in China in 1860–62 helping to put down the Taiping Rebellion in order to safeguard the city of Shanghai which was a flourishing port used by the British.

After some years in England Gordon was invited to take on the Governorship of the Sudan, – this was just the sort of impossible job that Gordon relished. One of his first tasks (in 1874) was to put down a revolt in Darfur Province. He mounted a camel, rode alone across 85 miles of blazing desert direct to the enemy camp. His commanding presence and single-mindedness caused the whole rebel host to obey his command to disband.

Gordon was brought up in a religious household, but he disliked the Church of England and declined confirmation. He developed a mystic sense and in letters to his devout sister Augusta we see the beginning of his obsession with death; longing for delivery from this weary world so that he could go to his 'glorious home'. He threw himself into working to relieve suffering and took homeless boys into his house to feed, clothe and educate them then attempt to get them into the Royal Navy.

In 1884 he was summoned back to the Sudan where an Islamist extremist Muhammad Ahmed 'The Mad Mahdi' was leading a rebellion. Gordon arrived in Cairo and on 18 February was in Khartoum. His orders were to withdraw the Egyptian and British personnel back to Egypt, but he refused to leave the native Sudanese to their likely massacre at the hands of the Mahdi's men. 2,500 people were evacuated, but on 18 March the siege began.

It was not until 5 August that Gladstone reluctantly agreed that an expedition should be sent to Khartoum, but it was October before the relief force started up the Nile under Lord Wolseley. The journey was painfully slow and a sense of urgency was lacking because the few messages received from Gordon did not suggest that the situation was critical. The first of 10,000 rescuers arrived on 28 January 1885 but two days earlier the Mahdi's soldiers had burst into the Palace and beheaded Gordon. His body was never found.

Gordon was an eccentric who spurned social life.[1] He was the complete misfit and had no interest in women which has made some suggest that he was a repressed homosexual. There is no evidence of this.

George Joy's painting of the General facing his murderers is now famous, and Charlton Heston learnt to ride a camel so that he could star as Gordon in the film *Khartoum* (1966).

[1] Anthony Nutting, *Gordon* (1966), p. 187.

The Very Revd Richard Church (1815–1890)

Lib's portrait of the Dean of St Paul's,
30 January 1886

'St Paul's'

He had always been a blind and ardent worshipper of Mr Gladstone and was by him brought to London in 1871 to be Dean of St Pauls with £2,000 a year.[1] He is a ripe scholar, a thoughtful and graceful writer, a moderate preacher, popular with the clergy, retiring in manner, a staunch friend, and an unsparing controversialist. He has declined a Bishopric.

The son of a wine merchant, he spent ten years of his childhood in Italy and came to love that country. He was sent to a strict evangelical school in Bristol then was admitted in 1832 to Wadham College, Oxford where he took first-class honours in 1836. He was elected a Fellow of Oriel in 1838 and was ordained the following year. He was drawn to the Tractarians and as a Proctor vetoed a proposal to censure the Tracts publicly, and received a letter of thanks from 500 members of the University. He was very happy at Oriel, writing to his mother on 1 August 1845:

> I wish that I could persuade you that Oxford is a very enjoyable place in the Long Vacation. One is very quiet with one Fellow, one cat, one dog, and one jackdaw with clipped wings, for one's companions; and when I am in the sulks, I can go to a friend who

[1] Approximately £200,000 in 2012.

lives just out of town, and all but in the country, at the Observatory, and smoke a cigar with him, and look at Jupiter and Saturn through his telescopes.[2]

This friend was almost certainly Newman, and two months later Church was told of his conversion which was 'intensely painful', and it was 14 years before they met again.

In January 1853 he accepted the small living of Whatley in Somerset and was married in that July to Helen Frances Bennett. He found the minds of his rural parishioners somewhat impenetrable but stayed at his post. In 1871 he accepted, most reluctantly, Gladstone's insistence that he go to the deanery of St Paul's.

Fortunately Gladstone had ensured that two High Church canons were at hand to help – Gregory and Liddon. The scholarly and genial Lightfoot and the courteous Claughton made up what is rare for St Paul's – a united chapter instead of 'an odd assortment of stray goods, contradictory specimens each of which had been specially selected in order to neutralise the others'. To them in 1884 was added Henry Scott Holland, liberal in politics and in religion. Church moaned that the Deanery was 'gloomy and like a prison, shut up between high walls',[3] but stayed 19 years.

A settlement had to be reached with the Ecclesiastical Commission, and in 1872 the Commission agreed to provide an annual income of £18,000 and a one-off

---

[2] Mary Church, *Life and Letters of Dean Church* (1894), p. 59.
[3] Today it is lived in by the Bishop of London.

payment of £30,000 for capital expenditure in return for the transfer of the cathedral's properties to the Commissioners. Amongst other improvements a choir school was built and a new peal of bells was installed. Choral communions were introduced on Sundays and Saints' days and daily communions began in 1877. The high standard of worship meant that angry protestants organised demonstrations, and at Easter 1883 an agitator rushed at the altar but his cries were stifled by the brawny Gregory who stuffed a handkerchief into his mouth.[4]

One of the finest preachers in England, Church was regarded in 1882 as a possible successor to Archbishop Tait, but his health made it out of the question. On 10 December 1890 early in the morning and quite quietly he died, and his body was taken to Whatley to be buried.

[4]   D. Keene, A. Burns and A. Saint, *St Paul's* (2004), pp. 90 – 91.

30

Edmund Sturge (1808–1893)

Spy's caricature, 20 November 1886

'A Quaker'

No kindlier, simpler, gentler, more upright and honourable
a soul ever informed a human body than that which is
enveloped in the Quaker outside of Mr Sturge. He is a
good, honest creature. He is the brother of that Mr Sturge
who went to St Petersburg thirty years ago to endeavour to
persuade the Russian Czar not to engage in the Crimean
War, and, like his brother was a Birmingham manufacturer.
He owned a large portion of the Island of Montserrat and
made chemicals; Fortune smiled upon him in commerce. His
remarkable but unobtrusive presence very constantly recalls,
in the Lobby of the House of Commons, those Quaker
characteristics of dress and gentleness which Mr Bright
forswore forty years ago, and it is always prompted by a
desire to do good to some fellow creature which all too rarely
meets with success, and not always with attention. He is a
good honest creature.

Edmund was born near Bristol, the youngest of ten
children. After school he joined his brother in business
and when their father returned in 1837 from visiting
the West Indies, he helped distribute his report on the
condition of slaves. He himself was part proprietor of
estates in the island of Montserrat and was therefore
especially knowledgeable about the condition of negroes.
In 1840, he joined the newly-formed British and Foreign

Anti-Slavery Society and later became its Secretary then Chairman. After he retired he regularly lobbied Parliament on the Society's business, and it was there that he was seen by Spy.

In 1841 Edmund married Lydia Albright who was also a campaigner for human rights. They had five children.

Spy referred to Sturge as 'a curious anomaly – a Puritan Beau'. [1] Owing to illness Sturge lost all his hair which meant for the rest of his life he had to wear a wig; to begin with his friends did not recognise him. He had a dry sense of humour and loved to tell anecdotes including that of a Quaker who was admitted to York prison. In silence he sat opposite the governor who eventually asked what he was thinking about. He said that he had been thinking of the Friends' precept, ' Whatsoever thy hand findeth to do, do it with thy might,' and forthwith he struck the governor violently. [2]

Edmund Sturge died aged 84 on 28 June 1893, at Charlbury.

---

[1] Ward, *Forty Years of Spy*, p. 243.
[2] William Tallack, *Reminiscences of Edmund Sturge* (1905).

31

The Revd Joseph Leycester Lyne
(1837–1908)

Ape's caricature, 9 April 1887

'Father Ignatius'

In 1862 being then five and twenty he believed himself to have had a call to restore Monasticism in England...He adopted himself into the Order of St Benedict. These assumptions were viewed with much disfavour and disapproval by the religious world and provoked amusement in the irreligious world. He went to Llanthony and invited novices male and female to take the vows. The Bishops of the Church of England inhibited him from preaching in their churches and refused all sanction to his monasticism.

He has a melodious voice and refined manners but he is not gifted with the power of organisation or with a strong common sense, and he is neither a great theologian nor a great preacher. He has some learning, great enthusiasm and much oratory; and he flings himself about, both morally and physically with such recklessness of consequences that he rarely fails to attract attention.

In 1856 Lyne was accepted as a divinity student by Trinity College at Glenalmond in Scotland but illness forced him to leave the college and he unsuccessfully attempted to found a monastery in Plymouth, then Ipswich, then Norwich. He had been made deacon in 1860 and his insistence on wearing a monk's habit infuriated many including his father who disliked his 'monastic fiddlesticks'. Lyne failed to realize that Benedict in his day had chosen the habit because it was the humblest form of working-class dress.[1]

In 1865 there were newspaper reports of a 'Norwich Scandal' featuring an inappropriate relationship between a novice monk and a young boy in the care of the monastery. Father Ignatius moved to London where, with the help of his female supporters, he established another Benedictine monastery in a house at Laleham, near Staines. In 1867–8 he was allowed to preach at St Edmund the King in the City of London where he delighted in attacking money-kings, but violence ensued and Bishop Tait of London was not impressed, refusing to priest him.

It was now time for a move to the countryside and he visited the ruined Llanthony Abbey in the Black Mountains in Wales near Abergavenny. Ignatius acquired a tract of mountainside above Capel-y-ffin, and began building a monastery. Four years later controversy flared up again when he accepted a seventeen year old boy as a novice. His parents went to law and the 'kidnapped Ward of Chancery' was returned home.

A Syrian prelate, Mar Timotheos, Metropolitan for the Old Catholics in America, visited Llanthony in 1898 and ordained Ignatius. The Metropolitan turned out to be a fraud, but Ignatius thought his ordination valid. No one else did, and in one stroke he had alienated his Anglican friends. The truth was that Ignatius always wanted to be in charge, and rarely listened to the opinions of others. During his life he had many psychosomatic illnesses,

[1]   Arthur Calder-Marshall, *The Enthusiast* (1962), p.68.

and alternated between soaring euphoria and abysmal despair.[2]

Ignatius died on 15 October 1908. The *Church Times* commented that 'no one was less monastic, less capable ... of following the rule of St Benedict. At no point did the spirit of obedience which is the first duty of the monk appear; at no time did he show himself capable of living with and working with others.'

[2] *Ibid.* p. 145.

32

The Revd James Joynes (1824–1908)

Spy's cartoon, 16 July 1887

'Jimmy'

He is honoured by Etonians with the title of 'Jimmy', and with a popularity such as has seldom been extended by boys to one whose mission has consisted in inflicting mental and corporeal anguish upon them. He is old fashioned in his notions, has a pious horror of modern innovations, has handled the birch with an unsparing hand, and has usually accompanied his stripes either with a grim word of warning or a biting jest addressed to the victim at the block; so that he has left a lasting impression on many generations of little boys.

After having gained the Newcastle Scholarship, he became an Assistant-Master at Eton. Subsequently to this he became a Fellow of Trinity College, Cambridge; and, in 1878, he returned to become Lower Master. Little is now known of this gentleman, but he would not be pleased to know that his proclivities feature in a pornographic novel written in 2000 about the poet Swinburne's time at Eton when Joynes was 'his dear old tutor'. Swinburne became a seasoned and unapologetic flagellist directly as a result of his schoolboy experiences at Eton.

A.C. Benson, who was at Eton, thought that Ward's caricature was true to life – 'pointing with an air at once sinister and pastoral to the flogging block; the half-closed eyes with their dull shadows, the big devouring mouth, give the picture a grim quality'.

33

The Rt Hon and Most Revd Edward Benson, (1829–1896)

Spy's cartoon of the Archbishop, 30 July 1887

'The Primate'

Benson, an undergraduate at Trinity College, Cambridge, was 23 when he proposed to his second cousin, Minnie (later Mary) Sidgwick in 1853. She was 12, so her mother suggested waiting a while but Minnie tied a lover's knot in her handkerchief and gave it to him. Edward returned to Cambridge then joined the staff at Rugby School at the invitation of the headmaster, Dr Goulburn who had succeeded Tait in 1849. Minnie's family bought a house in Rugby and Edward moved in with them. The 'engagement' was kept a secret. Edward became her unofficial tutor because he wanted his future wife to be educated and refined in accordance with his wishes.[1]

In January 1854 Edward was ordained despite being unable to answer a single question put to him by the Bishop of Manchester's chaplain. In 1859 Edward accepted the headmastership of Wellington College, a new public school erected in memory of the Duke. This gave him a good income, so at last the engagement was made public and Edward, now 29, and Minnie, now18, were married on 23 June by Dr Frederick Temple, the new Headmaster at Rugby. Benson at Wellington was a strict disciplinarian, severe and terrifying; he was a great

---

[1] I am greatly indebted to a recent splendid biography of Mary by Rodney Bolt, *As Good as God, as Clever as the Devil* (2011).

beater. A very handsome man, he could, however, be emotional and his eyes often filled with tears.

In 1876 he was offered the bishopric of the new diocese of Truro; he told Joseph Lightfoot the annual stipend of £3,000 (approximately £293,000 in 2012) was inadequate. When Tait died in 1882 Benson moved to Lambeth.

Edward suffered from bouts of melancholy and depression for most of his life partly caused no doubt by his unusual marriage, but also by the death of his eldest son Martin, a schoolboy of only 17. Having studied and written about St Cyprian, he had a high view of episcopacy, and felt that the bishops should provide a united front. Their meetings together should be given top priority, and he sent a severe rebuke to his close friend John Wordsworth, Bishop of Salisbury, who once excused himself because of a prior engagement. Earlier in his ministry he had questioned the Church's links with the State, but now changed his mind. If disestablishment happened he said he would 'head a revolt, seize the principle agitators and hang them at Lambeth out of the windows'. Accordingly he sat regularly in the Lords although found it 'a terrible place'. It has 'a conviction of the infallibility of laymen ...on all sacred subjects.'

All the Benson children were 'fiercely eccentric and unpermissably gifted'. Arthur, a Cambridge don and then Master of Magdalene College for ten years, wrote the words for 'Land of Hope and Glory'; Edward wrote the Mapp and Lucia novels; Maggie was a famous Egyptologist and Hugh an eccentric Roman Catholic priest. None were the marrying sort which is perhaps not surprising because their mother was a lesbian. All her life she had passionate relationships with women, and, after her husband's death, she set up a household with Lucy Tait, daughter of the Archbishop. The family wrote many books, mainly about themselves.

In 1896 Benson and Mary, stayed at Hawarden for a weekend with the Gladstones and enjoyed discussions with the Great Man, but at mattins in the local church on the Sunday morning the Archbishop collapsed and died. His funeral at Canterbury was on 16 October.

34

The Revd Ernest John Heriz Smith MA (1851–1911)

Hay's drawing, 28 January 1888

'Pembroke'

In 1873 Smith took a Second Class in the Classical Tripos and a First Class in the Theological; and being a double honourman, was naturally elected a Fellow of Pembroke. Subsequently he achieved the Dean, had the Proctor thrust upon him, and developed into Pembroke College of which he is the soul. Sincere in his work, generous in his friendship, and the leading spirit among the undergraduates, both in the schools and on the river, he has combined, with a success hitherto unequalled, the characters of Dean, Proctor, and Mr. Smith, each one of which is more popular than the other two.

It is on the River that Mr. Smith has achieved his greatest glory. There is no figure better known between Jesus Lock and Baitsbite than that of the Dean in his light and dark blue blazer, animating the toils of the fifth boat.

Smith never rowed in the Boat Race or at Henley but he is the first rower in *Vanity Fair*. Through men like Smith 'the Christian ethic became very deeply imbued in the sport of rowing at the club level throughout the country,' wrote historian Neil Wigglesworth, 'being disseminated and consolidated by seemingly endless supplies of ordained oarsmen coming down from Oxford and Cambridge colleges, settling into their new parishes and preaching a combination of rowing technique and religious virtue.'

He retired in 1896 to hold the college benefice at Tarrant Hinton in Dorset. At Pembroke he started a semi-religious society called the Companions of St John, whose members wore a belt of sash under their clothes and thus were popularly known as 'the belly-banders'.

36

Edward King (1829–1910)

Spy's drawing of the Bishop of Lincoln,
13 September 1890

'A Persecuted Bishop'

For ten years he was the moving power of that Ritualistic centre whence his influence gradually made itself felt throughout the Church, but ... he was unable to escape persecution; so that two years ago he began to be charged with divers heresies and idolatries ... yet he is as broad in his mind as he is rigidly conservative in his ritual. He is a courteous, kindly man, whose face, with its benignant, winning smile is the fair index to his character; and withal, he is simple and very honest ... he has a fine presence, a striking figure, and an engaging manner which is natural, and not clerically assumed ... Men listen to him; women adore him; and children love him. He is a power not a fashion.

King was pre-eminently a pastor as I was often told in my teens by two sisters who knew him and an Evangelical parson who owed his vocation to him.

King graduated from Oriel College, Oxford and was ordained in 1854 by Samuel Wilberforce, who four years later invited him to become chaplain and lecturer at Cuddesdon Theological College. He was principal from 1863 to 1873.

In February 1873 Gladstone, who knew of King's work because his son had been at Cuddesdon, offered him the Chair of Moral and Pastoral Theology at Oxford, which was joined with a canonry of Christ Church. This surprised many because he was not an academic, and Archbishop Tait tried to veto the appointment. King was welcomed by the students who hung a cassock from a lamppost outside his rooms. The new canon spent much time in spiritual direction and hearing confessions; Pusey was scandalised that his maid went to him – 'anyone can hear her simple confession'. King spoke French, German and Italian fluently and greatly enjoyed his walking holidays in Switzerland each summer with the students.

In 1885 he became Bishop of Lincoln and three years later the Church Association charged him with various ritual offences. The case dragged on for nearly four years and obviously caused King much distress. Benson, the Archbishop of Canterbury, heard the evidence in Lambeth Library with five episcopal assessors, and seemed to relish the mixture of drama and dogma. The Bishop of Oxford (Stubbs) who declared 'this is not a court but an Archbishop sitting in his library', spent most of the time writing comic verse. Eventually the Archbishop gave his judgement – the Bishop must not make the sign of the cross at the absolution and blessing. King obeyed this for the rest of his life.

King's pastoral gifts were immense and he enjoyed being with all sorts of people. He regularly visited the condemned cell at Lincoln Jail to be with those about to die; he gave a dinner for the jockeys riding in the Lincolnshire Handicap. He disliked administration and depended on his archdeacons for this. One question has to be asked. Why did this man so full of God's loving concern for the poor never express the slightest suspicion that the existing social order was anything other than God-given? Canon Neville of Lincoln suggests that perhaps he felt change was not possible and, as someone remarked, his religion was a 'yon-side' one. He had little to say on the problems of this side.[1]

To King life was an adventure –'The ice is thin, but I think that we can get across. I mean to try myself, won't you come along?'[2] He is buried in the cloister garth of Lincoln Cathedral, and he has a place in the Church of England's calendar – on 8 March, the day of his death.

[1] Graham Neville, *Bishop King: Right Heart, Wrong Head* (1986).
[2] B. Randolph and J. Townroe, *The Mind and Work of Bishop King* (1918), p. 89.

37

The Revd Dr James Sewell
(1810–1903)

Spy's cartoon of the Warden of New College
Oxford, 5 April 1894

'The Shirt'

His early youth is a matter of ancient history. He was chosen Warden four and thirty years ago and having seen many generations of men, he still intelligently rules nearly two hundred and fifty undergraduates and a foundation whose endowment income is £19,047.[1] The success of the College is greatly due to the human sympathy and the quiet dignity of the venerable Wykehamist who is its Head. He is a rare specimen (in these degenerate days) of the perfect gentleman but is also one of the kindest and gentlest creatures in the world; who probably (even in contentious Oxford) has no enemy that dare speak ill of him openly.

Sewell was born at Newport, Isle of Wight, educated at Winchester College and New College Oxford, of which he became a Fellow in 1830, and, apart from a few months as a curate at Hursley in Hampshire, remained there all his life, becoming a Tutor, Bursar then in 1860 Warden. During his time the College changed from being a small, close, conservative corporation limited to former pupils of Winchester College to be a large liberal-minded non-Wykehamist institution.

Spy went to Oxford and stayed at The Mitre to 'stalk' Sewell for several days, and although he sat next to him

---

[1] £2,031,242 in 2011.

in chapel he felt he had not 'sufficiently impressed his features upon my memory', so on two occasions watched him take his early morning walk. 'I saw him come out in all the glory of his beautiful white collar and cravat (which had earned him the nickname of *The Shirt*) and a red handkerchief, as usual, hanging from the pocket of his coat tail.[2]

Though himself instinctively conservative, Sewell determined that it was his duty to support the wishes of the majority of Fellows, with the result that New College led the way in the general reform movement, and from being one of the smallest became the second largest college in Oxford. He was Vice-Chancellor 1874–78.

A timid bachelor, Sewell had to live in a house provided in 1379 although it had been extended when celibacy was no longer required at the Reformation. Nothing was spent by Sewell on its 16 bedrooms, grand reception rooms and servants' quarters.

At the time of the Relief of Mafeking in 1899 the bells of every college except New College were rung, and angry students demanded why. 'When I was a boy,' said Sewell, I was walking with my aunt when news of Waterloo arrived. The bells of New College were not rung then and I see no reason to ring them now.' When it was suggested that baths be installed, he commented, 'What do they need baths for? They are only here for eight weeks at a time'.

He died in his ninety-third year, having been Warden of New College for 43 years, and was interred in the College

---

[2] Leslie Ward, *Forty Years of Spy* (1915), pp.220 – 1.

cloisters. Sewell had given away a great deal during his lifetime so only left £3,000. (Approximately £309,000 in 2012.)

38

Her Majesty the Queen Empress (1819–1901)

Guth's cartoon of the 78-year-old Victoria,
17 June 1897

'À Cimiez –Promenade matinale'

Victoria appeared only once in *Vanity Fair* and the occasion was her Diamond Jubilee. Jean Baptiste Guth portrays her as an old lady – tired, in decline but still a considerable character. She was visiting Cimiez near Nice in the south of France. Jehu's commentary was sycophantic:

Brought up in a stately manner so secluded as to be almost unintelligible in these newer days, the young Princess was unknown when she succeeded to the Throne just 60 years ago. She has constantly proved herself a greater Sovereign than Elizabeth: wiser, gentler, nobler, under harder conditions. For her hard work Her Majesty relinquished the more ornamental part of her duties; and with an industry of which her people are little aware, she has ever since devoted herself to the government of a mighty Empire with a success that has altogether left nothing to be desired.

Victoria's father, the Duke of Kent, had died when she was only eight months old so her mother was determined that she should be prepared for her high station in life, and she taught her religion. 'Sitting in the pew every Sunday morning, the child of six was seen listening in rapt attention to the clergyman's endless sermon, for she was to be examined upon it in the afternoon'.[1] No wonder she later forebade long sermons. The Duchess asked two bishops[2] to advise on her education telling them that her eleven-year-old daughter had 'religion at her heart'. They found that the Princess 'displayed an accurate knowledge of the most important features of Scripture, History and of the leading truths and precepts of the Christian Religion as taught by the Church of England'. This was probably due to her tutor, George Davys, a simple, safe parson who wrote improving tales featuring Will Wise, Ralph Ragged and Mary Manage. He was later rewarded with the Bishopric of Peterborough.[3]

Victoria succeeded to the throne on 20 June 1837, and from the moment of her coronation a year later she was certain that as 'head' of the Established Church she had a responsibility for its welfare and in particular the choice of its leaders. She kept herself well informed about matters spiritual and knew most of the interesting clerics of her reign. She recognised that the Prime Minister had the right to nominate men for vacant bishoprics, but her own advisors such as Deans Wellesley and Davidson were usually consulted early in the negotiations.

She was a Protestant and was always conscious of her Coronation oath to 'maintain the Protestant Reformed Religion established by law'. She loathed Roman Catholicism and was horrified by its growth during her reign. 'The Pope was never so powerful and the Queen is

---

[1] G. Barnett Smith, *Life of HM Queen Victoria* (1887), pp.21 – 2.
[2] Blomfield of London and Kaye of Lincoln.
[3] Malcolm Johnson, *Bustling Intermeddler?* (2001).

quite determined to do *all* in her power to prevent this'.[4] She was greatly offended when Cardinal Wiseman told his faithful to pray first for the Pope then the Queen. It was 'a *direct* infringement of my prerogative'. She was probably spiritually happier north of the Border where, much to the horror of the *Church Times*, she received communion at the Presbyterian Crathie church. Towards the end of her life a young curate asked Sir Henry Ponsonby for advice about a sermon he was to preach. 'It doesn't much matter *what* you say because Her Majesty is too deaf to hear; but on no account let it last for more than five minutes.'

There is no direct evidence that Victoria said 'We are not amused'. Indeed her granddaughter, Princess Alice of Athlone, whom I met in 1953, said that she had 'a tinkling laugh' and enjoyed jokes with the family – until a servant entered the room.

The Queen died at Osborne on 22 January 1901. She and Albert, who she married in 1840, had ten children and 42 grandchildren (of whom 34 survived to adulthood). She was interred beside Prince Albert in Frogmore Mausoleum in Windsor Great Park.

---

[4] F. Hardie, *The Political Influence of Queen Victoria*, p. 136.

39

The Revd William Spooner, (1844–1930)

Spy caricatures the 54 year old academic,
21 April 1898

'Spooner'

He is much younger than he looks ...Yet he seems to grow no older, so that new generations of men still find the same Spooner. He is a very learned gentle amiable modest Don. His chief flame to claim is his genius for metathesis.

Despite being a distinguished academic – Warden of New College (since 1903) and lecturer on philosophy and divinity at Oxford – he is remembered today for verbal confusions.

The Lord is a shoving leopard.

It is kisstomary to cuss the bride.

Re a Naval Review – This vast display of cattleships and bruisers.

To a student – You have hissed all my mystery lectures. Having tasted two worms you will leave by the next town drain.

All his life, as his biographer[1] points out, he looked like a white-haired baby. His appearance hardly changed. He was small, pink-faced and an albino, with a disproportionately large head and very short-sighted pale blue eyes. His nickname was thus 'The Child'. He was admitted to New College in1862 and was to stay

[1] William Hayter, *Spooner, a Biography* (1977).

there for 62 years. In 1878 he married Frances, daughter of Harvey Goodwin, Bishop of Carlyle. He called her Frank or 'Madonna' so the Madonna and Child had seven children, although two died in infancy and one was an invalid.

Having been ordained priest in 1875, he felt 'that Anglicanism taking it all in all is for Englishmen at any rate the best working hypothesis that has yet been invented. It is less repelling, meagre, unprogressive, unhistorical than Calvinism; more reasonable, liberal, and capable of greater progress than Romanism, even if it wants the authority of its pretensions'.

When Spooner arrived at New College it was a lazy, snobbish institution, but when he left he and the Fellows, after a period of stress, had made it a more modern, cosmopolitan, and prosperous place.

He could be rather absent-minded. One story tells of him inviting a don to tea 'to welcome Stanley Casson, our new archaeology Fellow'. 'But, sir, I *am* Stanley Casson.' 'Never mind, come all the same.' Another story tells of Spooner preaching about St Paul. When he left the pulpit he returned and told a bewildered congregation, 'Did I say Aristotle? I meant St Paul.'

To make a sketch for the caricature Ward went in a borrowed cap and gown to one of Spooner's lectures but was not spotted because of Spooner's poor eyesight. An undergraduate said, 'Don't worry, I'll tell him you are my governor'.

There are not many people whose surnames have given a word to the English language and there is evidence that Spooner did not enjoy his reputation for verbal metathesis, or the re-ordering of words, and once said to his formidable wife, 'Oh! Have I said another of those things again?' He resigned in December 1924 and moved with his wife to a north Oxford house. He died on 29 August 1930 and was buried at Grasmere. No doubt he was grattered and flatified by his appearance in *Vanity Fair*.

40

Sir Walter Phillimore (1845–1929)

Spy's cartoon, 24 November 1898

'A Judicial Churchman'

It is useful for a barrister of eminence to have been born to a Judge ... if only because a Lord Chancellor is able to select him as being of the judicial caste. But Sir Walter Phillimore had more virtues than that of an honoured name; he was himself a learned, honourable and courteous gentleman who had long had a fine practice in the Courts of Admiralty.

He is also a pronounced High Churchman who so greatly objects to divorce (on principle) that, as a Counsel, he declined to practise in the Divorce Court. Altogether he is an ornament to his profession who has deserved his success.

The son of a distinguished judge, Sir Robert, he was educated at Westminster School and Christ Church, Oxford then become a Fellow of All Souls. Called to the bar in 1868 he joined the western circuit and as a devout Christian was often asked to be counsel for the defence in church ritual cases. In one case he ruled that a nonconformist clergyman could not be titled 'the Rev' on his tombstone. The decision was upheld by his father but reversed by the Privy Council.

In 1874 Phillimore stood before his father representing Fr Mackonochie in a case brought by the indefatigable Church Association. 'The great offender' among the ritualists was accused of erecting a confessional at St Alban Holborn and other offences already declared illegal by the Dean of the Arches such as having lighted candles on the holy table. The judge was unmoved by his son's eloquence and found Mackonochie guilty on all but one count and suspended him for six weeks. Mackonochie decided not to appeal; this was his fourth court appearance.[1]

In 1885 he succeeded to his father's baronetcy. He had been Chancellor of the Lincoln diocese since 1872 so in 1889 he was Counsel for Bishop King at his trial in Lambeth Palace. Phillimore told King that he was 'Your devoted friend and Chancellor'.

In December 1897 he was appointed a judge of the Queen's Bench division. It was thought that his sentences were too severe especially in sexual cases, but he mellowed as he got older. He was somewhat pedantic and precise in his ways and methods. From 1913 he was a Lord Justice of Appeal and a member of the Privy Council. Five years later he was raised to the peerage as Baron Phillimore.

A convinced Christian he joined the English Church Union in 1865 and was President in 1919. He was also Treasurer of Pusey House and one of the chief authors of the scheme for clergy pensions.[2]

A 1924 entry in Evelyn Waugh's diary relates that Phillimore was anxious about what sentence to pass in a sodomy trial over which he was presiding so consulted F.E. Smith the Lord Chancellor. 'Could you tell me, what do you think one ought to give a man who allows himself

---

[1]   B. Palmer, *Reverend Rebels*, pp.96 – 98.
[2]   DNB vol. 1922–30, Sankey p.677.

to be buggered?' Smith replied, 'Oh, thirty shillings or two pounds; anything you happen to have on you'.

In 1870 Phillimore married Agnes Lushington and they had four sons and three daughters. Aged 83 he died in 1929 in Kensington, where he had been Mayor 1909–11.

41

Robert Baden-Powell (1857–1941)

Drawl's cartoon of the General, 5 July 1900

'Mafeking'

His father being a parson and his mother an Admiral's daughter, he was naturally born a fighting man. He fought with his nurse; he fought at Charterhouse, and then he joined the 13th Hussars. He treats life like a joke.

He was summoned from Henley Regatta last year to the War Office. The Saturday afterwards he sailed for the Cape – to make the story of the Siege of Mafeking in circumstances which are known the world over.

He is a keen soldier who never misses an opportunity; he is full of courage; his recklessness is tempered with great wit; he has a very cheerful nature; he can rough it (or ruffle it) with the best, and altogether he is a lively fellow. He is an author who has been guilty of a valuable book on the art of scouting, of which art he is a master. He believes greatly in the virtue of a smile.

B-P, as he became known, was born in Paddington and his father died when the boy was only three. He was awarded a scholarship to Charterhouse, and his first introduction to scouting skills was stalking and cooking animals – and avoiding teachers – in the nearby woods, which were strictly out-of-bounds. He also played the piano and violin, was an ambidextrous artist of some talent, and enjoyed acting. Holidays were usually spent on yachting or canoeing expeditions with his brothers.

Having failed the entrance exams to Oxford he decided to enter the Army and served from 1876 until 1910 in India and Africa. In 1899, during the Second Boer War in South Africa, Baden-Powell as Commander successfully defended the town in the Siege of Mafeking. Surrounded by 8,000 Boers it lasted 217 days. Both sides were Christian so no killing took place on a Sunday; the English played polo. The siege was lifted on 16 May 1900, and Baden-Powell was promoted to Major-General and became a national hero. In 1910, now a Lieut-General, he decided to retire reputedly on the advice of Edward VII who said he should devote his time to Scouting.

B-P's religion was real, practical, and based on Christianity but open to other faiths. When asked where religion came into Scouting and Guiding he replied 'It does not come in at all, it is already there. It is a fundamental factor underlying them both'.

> Every Scout should have a religion ... Religion seems a very simple thing: First: Love and Serve God. Second: Love and serve your neighbour'.[1] 'Christ gave His life to show us that example, namely, to 'Be Prepared' – no matter what it costs to ourselves – to do the right thing for others. [2]

In 1911 Jehu wrote:

[1] *Scouting For Boys* (1908).
[2] *Adventuring To Manhood* (1936). See Association of Christians Through Scouting (ACTS) accessed 30 March 2012.

He has grasped the trite old saying that 'the boy is the father of the man' and set himself heart and soul to make the rising race alert for the facing of every possible contingency. He finds it necessary to continually disarm the idea that all his work in the cultivation of the Boy Scout is directed toward building up the raw material for the future British Army.

His *Scouting for Boys* was published in 1908 and two years later he and his sister Agnes founded the Girl Guides, and by 2011 Scouting and Guiding together had over 41 million members worldwide

Slim and spare in physique he was a man of simple tastes, tending to the austere. When he was aged 55 B-P married Olave Soames, aged 23, on 31 October 1912, at St Peter's Church in Parkstone, and over the next five years they had three children. He slept on an open verandah for most of his married life and in the early days found the physical side difficult, giving him intense headaches and disturbing dreams.[3]

Made a Baronet in 1922, he was later created Baron Baden-Powell, and was appointed to the Order of Merit in 1937. He lived his last years in Nyeri, Kenya, where he died and was buried in 1941.

[3] DNB, Allen Warren vol. 45, p. 116.

42

Winston Leonard Spencer Churchill
(1874–1965)

Spy's portrait of the future Prime Minister,
27 September 1900

'Winston'

The elder son of a very beautiful mother and a very able father ... has had a good deal of war-like experience. He is firm in his conviction and he has all the confidence that may be begotten of the union of Practical Experience with Quick Youth.

Being quick-witted, lithe, active and perhaps lucky he was able to escape from Pretoria in a manner which caused some sensation and made him the hero of the hour ... He can write and he can fight. He is something of a sportsman; who prides himself on being practical rather than a dandy; he is ambitious; he means to get on, and he loves his country. But he can hardly be the slave of any party.

In writing this about the 26-year-old Churchill, Jehu Junior was more prophetic than he realised. He was twice to cross the floor of the House of Commons, and his finest hour was in May 1940 when he became Prime Minister and led Great Britain to victory over the Axis powers. Hundreds of books have described his brilliant career so the story does not need re-telling here. After six years in opposition he returned to Downing Street in 1951 and stayed there until he retired in 1955.

It may seem that the Church mattered little to Winston but when he was at Harrow he wrote to his mother, 'Really I feel less keen about the Army every day.

I think the Church would suit me much better'. Later as a cavalry subaltern he mused, 'One of these days – perhaps – the cold bright light of science and reason will shine through the cathedral windows and we shall go out into the fields to seek God for ourselves'.

When he was in India aged 22 his close friend Violet Bonham Carter tells us that he decided to order books from England to read in the hot afternoons. He felt that he was ill-educated. 'What were Ethics? They had never been mentioned to me at Harrow or Sandhurst'. He was severely shaken by one book which said that at death 'we simply go out like candles', a prospect which did not appeal to him. He then passed through what he called 'a violent and aggressive anti-religious phase which, had it lasted, might easily have made me a nuisance'. But his 'poise was restored during the next few years by frequent contact with danger'. Bonham Carter considers that he thought with his heart and felt with his mind.[1]

After he became Prime Minister Archbishop Lang found it difficult to get a word in edgeways when he went to lunch to discuss vacant bishoprics. Filling the vacancy at Ipswich and St Edmundsbury was hardly a priority when the Battle of Britain was raging in the skies.[2] Lang lamented that the Prime Minister 'knows almost nothing of the Church and its personalities'. He was responsible for appointing or translating 32 men to bishoprics,[3] and

[1] V Bonham Carter, *Winston Churchill as I knew him (1965)*, pp. 33, 34.
[2] Richard Brook was appointed. He confirmed me in 1951!
[3] These are carefully described in Palmer, *High and Mitred*, pp. 214 – 233.

apparently enjoyed moving bishops around as in a game of chess.

Archbishop Lang retired in1942, aged 78, and was apprehensive that the Prime Minister would not appoint the obvious candidate, William Temple of York, because he was too left-wing. Churchill realised Temple should be translated because, in his famous phrase, Temple 'was the only half-a-crown article in a sixpenny bazaar'.

Winston told Archbishop Geoffrey Fisher that he was not a pillar of the Church. 'I might claim, perhaps, to be a buttress – a flying buttress, on the outside'.

We must thank Churchill for the appointment of Michael Ramsey to Durham in 1952. Fisher put three names forward with no preference. However, Churchill decided to take 'an exciting gamble'.

Churchill must have the last word. When asked later in life about his death, he replied 'I am ready to meet my Maker; whether He is ready to meet me is another matter'. He died in 1965 and was given a State Funeral.

43

Arthur Foley Winnington-Ingram (1858–1946)

Spy's portrait, 23 May 1901

'London'

Loved and respected in East London. Sympathetic and unpatronising, hard working and humble minded; and as full of true learning as he is empty of priggishness. He is really free from neo-Apostolic side. He is on his way to Canterbury, but he might be side-tracked to York.

Ingram was educated at Marlborough College and Keble College, Oxford. Here he fell under the spell of Edward King who became his spiritual father and they remained friends. Later when they were both in the House of Lords King told him if because of deafness he could not hear a debate he would follow him in voting. After ordination as a priest in 1885 he did his curacy at Shrewsbury but only stayed eighteen months because the Bishop of Lichfield made him his chaplain.

In 1889 he was persuaded to be Head of Oxford House, Bethnal Green where 30 men from the University lived and worked among the very poor. 'Have plenty going on' he told them, 'it's idle hands that break up furniture ... Cater for body, mind and spirit' – boxing, dumbbells, reading, writing and a voluntary Bible class. Eight years in Bethnal Green prepared him to be Bishop of Stepney, and in 1901 Bishop of London.

Bishop Creighton who appointed him to Stepney told him, 'I choose you not because I think you will do it well, but because I cannot think of anyone who would do it better ... Don't ask me what my suffragans do; they go where they like, do what they like, and say what they like, and I get the blame'.[1]

During the Great War he threw himself into supporting the war effort and visited the troops on both the Western Front and at Salonica and the Grand Fleet. Known as Uncle Arthur, he was no Pacifist, and some thought his philosophy too simplistic – 'What would you do if someone attacked your sister?' His sermons could be jingoistic and he enjoyed wearing army uniform. Ian Hislop in a TV programme referring to the Great War said recently, 'The C of E wasn't the limp and liberal institution it is today; it was much more muscular. Some of the sermons by the likes of Bishop Winnington-Ingram were blood-curdling.'

The Bishop had three baths a day, and preaching to an East End congregation who probably only had a weekly bath if they were lucky, he told them that after a bath he felt rosy all over. A voice shouted out, 'Who is Rosie?'

[1]   S.C.Carpenter, *Winnington-Ingram* (1949), p. 61.

43 continued ....

In his lighter moments

Bishop Winnington-Ingram aged 54
WH's caricature, 25 May 1912

Recreation was important to Ingram; it kept him fit for his busy life. Tennis in the courts of Fulham Palace, his summer home, or better still golf were his favourites. At the Bath Club his opponent for squash was often the Prince of Wales.

His Christmas children's parties, held each year at London House in St James's Square, were described to me by Miss Margaret Marr in the 1970s. She and all the diocesan clergy children were invited. Brakes and cabs would arrive from all over London and after a huge tea there were games with the Bishop leading them, a child among children. Standing on a chair he would shout 'Do you love me?' The reply was deafening.

Administration was not his strong point. In 1939 when Cyril Garbett, Bishop of Winchester, visited the 81 year old Ingram who was now retired and living in a Bournemouth hotel, he noted in his diary:

> He now looks old and is very talkative ... He always told us at bishops' meetings that in London there was no disobedience, but this was only because there were no rules to obey. He has left the diocese in a condition of ecclesiastical chaos, every man a law unto himself ... A heart of pure gold.[2]

On 22 May 1946, Winnington-Ingram was taken ill while playing golf and he died four days later in Upton-upon-Severn, Worcestershire. His body was cremated and the

---

[2] Charles Smyth, *Cyril Forster Garbett* (1959), p.184.

ashes placed in Upton church. The public funeral was on
7 June at St Paul's Cathedral.

44

The Revd Cecil Legard (1843–1918)

C.B.'s portrait, 11 July 1901

'A Judge'

He was born to a good old Yorkshire stock eight and fifty years ago; but he is still quite a young man of very wholesome life, who loves the Country, his County, and his Parish in crescendo scale. He loves his fellow-creatures, and he loves that most beautiful work of God, a horse; and he is believed to be a good judge of both.

There is not a soul in his parish who is not devoted to him. An English gentleman and a good, sound, square parson of the best, if not the newest, school.

A hunting clergyman and a steeplechaser, he was educated at Magdalene College, Cambridge, and held a number of livings before becoming rector of Cottesbrooke, Northamptonshire, in 1887. He was also a judge of dogs as the cartoon suggests.

In 1873, he married Emily Hall. Peter Watkin's book *The Soul of Wit* refers to him thus:

> Snobbish and enthusiastic he took on the responsibility for the publication of the Fox Hound Kennel Stud Book. He would refer to heaven as 'that beautiful grass country where there's always a scent and never a blank day'. His valuable service to masters and huntsmen did not however prevent them from noticing his extreme partiality towards

196

the aristocracy, and he was always known among them as 'His Oiliness'.

He became a baronet in about 1910 on the death of an older brother, Charles.

45

HM King Edward VII (1841–1919)

Spy's drawing of Edward VII, 19 June 1902

'Tum Tum' took an interest in the Established Church and attended worship regularly, sometimes with Queen Alexandra at All Saints Margaret St. When he was eleven Dr Becker who taught him German queried Prince Albert's harsh, rigorous educational plan for the boy and commented that 'the main features in the Prince of Wales's character are a profound religious feeling, a great straightforwardness, and a sense of truth'. With great courage, Becker warned Albert that the outbursts of blind, destructive rage were a direct result of being subjected to a system which caused huge stress and at times 'total prostration and collapse'.

He was confirmed by Archbishop Sumner at Windsor on 1 April 1858 and his biographer notes 'an unclouded and humble religious faith remained with him always and was an immense source of strength'.[1] In that year his mother agreed that he was 'good, warm and affectionate ...but idle and weak'. He was never to be close to her and after Albert's death the rift widened.

In 1861, Edward transferred from Oxford to Trinity College, Cambridge where he was tutored in history by Charles Kingsley whose lectures he enjoyed. Determined to enter the army, the prince spent that summer at an

[1] Philip Magnus, *King Edward the Seventh* (1964), pp. 10 – 14, 24.

army camp at the Curragh, near Dublin. There he met Nellie Clifden, an actress, who was smuggled into his tent by his friends. She was indiscreet and the story was soon round London, and Albert, who was furious, visited Cambridge to vent his anger. Shortly afterwards the Prince Consort died of typhoid fever, and Victoria blamed her son for his death. On 10 March 1863, Bertie married Princess Alexandra of Denmark.

Edward was a well-known womaniser and had mistresses throughout his married life, of which three were 'official' and with whom he was in love – Lillie Langtry, Daisy Warwick and Alice Keppel, the great grandmother of Camilla, Duchess of Cornwall. He became known as 'Edward the Caresser'.

His interests included gambling, country sports and horse racing. In 1896, his horse Persimmon won both the Derby and the St Leger and others of his horses won the Grand National, the 2,000 Guineas and Newmarket Stakes.

Having waited so long for his succession, he was determined to rule wisely and he will be particularly remembered for his influence on foreign affairs and military and naval matters. He spoke fluent German and French and his State Visit to Paris in 1903 was a huge success. He holidayed every year in Biarritz.

Bertie appeared several times in *Vanity Fair* and all the drawings and write-ups were deferential, although the first (in 1873) made the Prince look jauntily dissipated at Cowes; Jehu did congratulate him for not forming a Prince's Party. The new king was not as interested as his mother in ecclesiastical appointments; he once said, 'I do not mind what religion a man professes but I distrust him who has none'.[2]

His interest in episcopal appointments was also not as keen as his mother's, but he always made his views known to Archbishop Davidson whom he did not much care for – 'not a strong man either physically or morally'.[3]

Edward VII died on 6 May 1910 and his body was buried in the vault beneath St George's Chapel at Windsor on 20 May. Edward might not have always lived up to his faith but he never lost it.

[2] Giles St Aubyn, *Edward VII: Prince and King* (1979), p. 39.
[3] Palmer, *High and Mitred*, p.140.

Cosmo Gordon Lang, Bishop of Stepney (1864–1945)

Spy's portrait, 19 April 1906

'A Bishop of Decision'

A powerful speaker and preacher.

Born in Fyvie, Aberdeenshire the third son of a Church of Scotland minister, he was educated at Glasgow University and Balliol College, Oxford. He hoped to be a lawyer or politician but in the spring of 1889 he attended evening service in the country church at Cuddesdon and, in his own words, during the sermon heard 'a masterful inward voice' which told him, 'You are wanted. You are called. You must obey'. He immediately decided to be ordained and to attend Cuddesdon theological college on 'the holy hill'. He was confirmed by the saintly Edward King at Lincoln and began his training. His fellow students called him The Lord High Cosmopolitan. Probably gay, he was a solitary person but admitted he had 'a strong craving for affection'.

After ordination, now nearly 26, he went to Leeds where the staff were 'a very happy and merry party' although he found little in common with them, and they thought him aloof. Three years later he became Dean of Divinity at Magdalen College Oxford.

After only two years he accepted the living of St Mary, Portsea, a parish of 40,000 people with a huge church seating 2,000. Lang established his authority and the team of curates, never less than 14, lived in the large clergy house, (now an undertakers), or nearby and ate together. Thinking that he might be too High Church several parishioners aired their misgivings and one man wrote to the newspaper saying that the new vicar 'practised celibacy openly in the street'. He worked extremely hard during his five years and in 1898 was invited to preach before the Queen in the Isle of Wight. She liked him but thought that he should marry; he replied that he could get rid of his curates but that a wife was for life. He became a royal chaplain and assisted with Victoria's funeral arrangements.

Lang's rise to the episcopate was meteoric for aged only 37 he was consecrated Bishop of Stepney in 1901. The Socialists Will Crooks and George Lansbury became friends and with the latter he set up an organisation to help the unemployed. When Lang left Stepney he sent a considerable sum of money to Lansbury:

> I have always looked upon you as a comrade in my work ... I don't want to lose the link you have between the Church and Labour. I pray that God will use you for his Kingdom.[1]

In 1908 Asquith asked him to be Archbishop of York which surprised him as he did not know the Prime Minister, but Davidson thought him 'a man of first-rate ability, earnestness and strength'. He stayed in the Northern Province for 20 years, and greatly enjoyed his

---

[1]   Bob Holman, *Good Old George* (1990), p. 36.

relations with Davidson'. When he left in1928 Lang was the obvious choice as successor.

Insofar as anyone comes close to them, Lang formed friendships with the royal family, so in 1936 was much involved with the Abdication crisis. In 2012 Robert Beaken discovered letters at Lambeth written by Lang to Baldwin suggesting that 'HM is mentally ill, and that his obsession is due not to mere obstinacy but to a deranged mind. More than once in the past he's shown symptoms of persecution-mania'.[2]

Lang also told Baldwin that Edward had undergone treatment for alcoholism using hypnotism, though he had no evidence of this. As Primate he obviously had to oppose the marriage of the Supreme Governor of his Church to a divorcée but his tactics are suspect, and he made matters worse by broadcasting to the nation two days after the Abdication, the king's motive had been 'a craving for private happiness' that he had sought 'in a manner inconsistent with the Christian principles of marriage'. Gerald Bullett wrote:

> My Lord Archbishop, what a scold you are!
> And when your man is down, how bold you are!
> Of Christian charity how oddly scant you are!
> And, auld Lang swine, how full of cant you are!

When the Archbishop visited the new king, George VI, his wife and their two daughters, Elizabeth and Margaret

---

[2] Lang to Dawson, 6 December 1936, quoted in R. Beaken, *Cosmo Lang: Archbishop in War and Crisis* (2012).

Rose, he felt that he had woken from a nightmare and the sun was shining. His last official act, on 28 March 1942, was to confirm Princess Elizabeth who he had baptised in 1926. He resigned three days later and went to live at Kew where he confessed to being lonely. He died there on 5 December 1945 running to catch a train. After the Westminster Abbey funeral his ashes were taken to Canterbury Cathedral.

47

The Revd Frank Gillingham
(1875–1953)

Spy's cartoon, 15 August 1906

'Cricketing Christianity'

Appropriately enough he began his clerical career in 1899 at Leyton, the home of Essex cricket. Owing to his work there and to his duties as a Chaplain to the Forces at Tidworth, Mr Gillingham has only been able to turn out occasionally. The Essex team chaff him that he picks his wickets, but they know that he prefers to play when his aid is most required and that he has often got the county out of a tight corner. He cannot bowl, but the severest critic of Essex fielding- and there are such people about – could say nothing against Mr Gillingham's excellence in that department of the game. A great feature of his batting is that he succeeds on any wicket, and two or three weeks without practice seems to make no difference to his ability to get runs.

On one historic occasion he illustrated the elevating effect of fervency of spirit by dispatching from the pulpit a fireballon, which ascended to the ceiling, to the delight of the youthful congregation. He now lives with the South Wales Borderers on Salisbury Plain. He fancies himself somewhat in the mess kit. He is a fine preacher, but his reputation on the cricket field gives him a better chance of saving souls than would all the eloquence in the world.

Born in Japan in 1875 Gillingham studied at Dulwich College then received his degree at Durham. He was the BBC's first ball-by-ball commentator, and at Leyton on 14 May 1927 he broadcast four stints, totalling 25 minutes, on the Essex v. New Zealanders match. Picked largely because he was a former county cricketer who was 'a terrific preacher' according to T. N. Pearce, a former team-mate, he was not really suited to the confines of the BBC. The newspapers greeted the experiment with indifference. Gillingham continued to do the odd commentary until he infuriated Lord Reith, when he filled in time during a rain break at The Oval by reading the various advertisements round the ground.

Tall and powerfully built, he was a strong believer in hitting the ball hard in front of the wicket, and though he was first to admit that he was not at ease against spin, he dealt firmly with bowlers of pace. His best season for Essex was that of 1908 when he scored 1,033 runs, averaged 39.73 and hit four centuries. His highest innings was 201 against Middlesex at Lord's in 1904.

He served in France from August 1914 as Chaplain of the Forces, and was mentioned in Dispatches. From 1919 he served in various parishes, and in 1939 he became a royal chaplain. He died on 1 April 1953.

48

The Very Revd William Ralph Inge
(1860–1954)

WH's portrait, 31 January 1912

'The Genial Dean'

At Eton he addressed a group of headmasters and said that the subjects in the Public Schools were ill-chosen, the methods of teaching them were radically bad, they were pursued by the demon of examinations and the attention of the boys was more and more distracted by too many subjects.

Inge ('my name rhymes with sting') had a High Church upbringing which left him with an aversion to the fierce bigotry of the Oxford Movement. In his home the slightest concession to liberalism in theology was denounced. Inge, after Eton, went to King's College, Cambridge where he won a number of prizes as well as taking firsts in both parts of the classical tripos. In 1885 he had been made deacon, but his priesting was delayed for four years because of his religious doubts. He came to realise that a Church believing in miracles would be exposed to scientific criticism, so Christianity must focus on personal experience and mysticism. In 1907, he was given the Lady Margaret's Professor of Divinity chair. He married Kitty Spooner, niece of *the* Spooner, and she helped him overcome his crippling shyness. She was 'fanatically economical'.[1]

In 1911 Asquith made him Dean of St Paul's, saying that he wanted a learned, literary Dean. It was a slightly

[1]   D. Collins, *Partners in Protest* (1922), p. 72.

odd appointment because Inge hated choral music – 'Are we quite sure the deity enjoys being serenaded?' Daily services he thought 'dreary and interminable' and he was often seen reading a book in his stall. 'The noise gets on my nerves and interferes with consecutive thought.' Asked if he was interested in liturgiology the tone-deaf Dean replied that he was not, nor was he interested in philately and postage stamps'. Relations with the canons were not easy and he famously said that he felt like a mouse being watched by four cats. Then, as now, the Dean had no casting vote, so securing change was difficult.

In 1921 Inge became a regular contributor to the *Evening Standard*. It was, he thought, 'a vulgar little paper' but it paid well and made him one of the best known clerics in England. He had, he said, ceased to be a pillar of the Church, and was now two columns in a newspaper. His conservative, acerbic pieces infuriated many, and he was delighted to receive an angry letter from a lady who wrote, 'I am praying nightly for your death, it may interest you to know that in two other cases I have had great success'.

He disliked democracy which he thought would lead to mob rule, and he opposed state welfare provision which was subsidising the weak and feckless. He considered the shortage of servants was 'a matter of national importance'. Archbishop Davidson rebuked him for saying that the working class was breeding too fast and that the State should control which couples could procreate.[2]

---

[2] Matthew Grimley, DNB vol.29, p. 241.

After his retirement from the Deanery in September 1934 the Gloomy Dean, as he was then known, moved to Brightwell near Wallingford. Inge opposed war with Germany, admiring its strong government but condemning the tyranny of the Nazis.

He died at Brightwell Manor near Wallingford on 26 February 1954 aged 94, and on 2 March was buried in the village churchyard beside his wife and son.

49

Gilbert Keith Chesterton
(1874–1936)

Strickland's caricature, 21 February 1912

'G.K.C.'

He looks acts, feels, thinks and wishes to appear like Dr Johnson. He is a democrat of the democrats, and has never been mistaken for a titled 'toff'. There are many who can remember the time when he could be seen in Fleet St every day, when his flapping cloak, his broad-brimmed hat and his sword-stick were signs of the town, when he filled its taxicabs with his bulk and its taverns with his mountainous laughter.

His original intention was to become an artist, and he studied drawing in a more or less desultory fashion. Later he drifted into a publisher's office, and drifted out again; publishers found him more useful as an author than as a clerk. He has gone on producing novels, biographies, criticisms, volumes of verse, controversial books on politics and religion, and, incidentally, finding time for an immense journalistic output.

The enormous vitality which is the note of his work is the note also of his personality. He himself is at once just as genial and just as pugnacious as are his writings, and no man is easier to 'draw' either into public or private controversy.

Born in Campden Hill, Kensington, his father was a house-agent and the name is still seen on sign boards today. He went to St Paul's School then on to the Slade School of Art and University College London, but did not stay to get a degree from either of them. Aged 22 he worked for a publishing house for six years then became a freelance journalist. In 1900 he heard and was impressed by a speech of Hilaire Belloc, the Roman Catholic writer, and the two men became friends; Chesterton gained a mentor who was to shape his outlook on life. In 1902 Chesterton was given a weekly column in the *Daily News* and three years later he had a weekly column in *The Illustrated London News* which continued for the next 30 years.

David Cecil in his biography of Max Beerbohm writes 'at the turn of the century there rocketed up into the English literary empyrean a coruscating new luminary of wit and fancy' – GK.

> Enormous apparition. Head big for body – way of sinking head on chest. Like a mountain and a volcanic one – constant streams of talk flowing down – paradoxes flung up into the air – very magnificent ... a strain of sensitiveness and shyness.[1]

G.K. Chesterton was a devout Christian and most of his non-fiction writing deals with Christian theology. Some of his best known works of fiction are detective novels featuring the Catholic priest, Fr Brown moulded on his Yorkshire friend Fr O'Connor. In 1922 he was received into the Roman Catholic Church in a tin tabernacle in Beaconsfield. His wife Frances was in floods of tears throughout, and Fr O'Connor took her to a hotel for a stiff drink.[2]

[1] David Cecil, *Max* (1964), pp. 199 – 200.
[2] A.N. Wilson, *Hilaire Belloc* (1984), pp.249 – 50.

Chesterton wrote around 80 books, several hundred poems, and 200 short stories. He was a large man, standing 6 feet 4 inches and weighing around 21 stones. He rarely remembered where he was supposed to be going and would even miss the train that was supposed to take him there. It was not uncommon for him to send a telegram to Frances (who he had married in 1901) from some distant location writing such things as, 'Am at Market Harborough. Where ought I to be?'

At the outbreak of the Great War someone asked him, 'Why are you not out at the Front?' and GK replied 'Madam, if you go round to the side, you will see that I am'. In fact in the autumn of 1914 he was laid low with a very serious illness and he was in a coma until the following Easter. The bed broke under his vast bulk.[3]

Chesterton died on 14 June 1936, at his home in Beaconsfield, Buckinghamshire. The homily at his Requiem Mass in Westminster Cathedral was delivered by Monsignor Ronald Knox who said, 'All of this generation has grown up under Chesterton's influence so completely that we do not even know when we are thinking Chesterton'. Near the end of his life Pope Pius XI made him a Knight Commander with Star of the Papal Order of St Gregory the Great. The Chesterton Society has proposed that he be beatified, and in August 2013 the Bishop of Northampton appointed a priest to look into the matter.

[3] *Ibid.* p. 219.

50

The Revd Herbert Hensley Henson
(1863–1947)

WH's portrait of the future Bishop, 24 April 1912

'St Margaret's'

A short, spare clergyman with a tense, nervous manner and a most earnest tone of voice, not over strong and round. What words he speaks will cause you to think much and seriously. There are some who say that he is subversive, others hail him as a prophet. He enjoys his newspaper, his enviable position and his dog.

Henson's childhood was deeply unhappy; his mother died when he was six and his father was left with eight children so hired a nurse, but decided not to send them to school. Hensley fled into the library of the house and read adult books which impressed his schoolmates when at 14 he eventually entered the local Broadstairs Collegiate School. He found the place detestable, and later said that his life began when, thanks to the help of his stepmother, he matriculated at Oxford, and became a 'tosher', – unattached to any College. In his otherwise exhaustive three-volume memoirs *Retrospective of an Unimportant Life* he only devotes three pages to his first 18 years. He obtained a First Class in Modern History, and was elected to a Fellowship at All Souls in 1884. He was made a deacon by the Bishop of Oxford (Mackarness) in Cuddesdon church on 5 June 1887. Three months later he became Head of Oxford House in Bethnal Green and was so excited that he spent that afternoon riding around

London on the top of a bus. An academic at not yet 24, he was able to work pastorally among the poor and on a soapbox in Victoria Park speak about Christ's life.

At the end of 1888 he moved to Barking and built up a congregation who were attracted by his fiery sermons and public debates. (He was a supporter of the Temperance Movement and an opponent of Socialism.) The young Cosmo Lang thought that he had 'an unruly tongue' and feared his 'power of denunciation and sarcasm'.[1] He believed that the market must control wages and he attacked Christian Socialists for 'wooliness of thought and for being chaplains of King Demos'.[2] In 1900 he became rector of St Margaret's Westminster, which gave him a pulpit from which he could preach to members of Parliament. Two years later his vow of celibacy crashed and he married Ella Dennistoun, who complemented him, but their childlessness was the *greatest shadow*.

Shortly after the caricature appeared Henson became Dean of Durham and he moved into the Deanery which dates back to Norman times; the house required a staff of eight plus gardeners. By now Logic, the Aberdeen terrier sketched by WH, had won everyone's hearts and was an important member of the household, but soon after the dog mysteriously disappeared. The War was on, and Henson courageously condemned reprisal raids, and championed brave conscientious objectors.

The uproar surrounding Henson's consecration as Bishop of Hereford in 1917 (against the advice of Randall

[1] Lockhart, *Life of Cosmo Gordon Lang*, p. 76.
[2] Chadwick, *The Victorian Church Part 2*, pp. 282 – 3.

Davidson) and then his translation three years later to Durham focussed on his disbelief of the Virgin Birth and the bodily resurrection. Eventually he made a statement of faith which silenced his critics. He arrived at Durham just as 20 years of unemployment and unhappiness began in the coal industry. He soon showed that he admired the miners who existed on very small wages, but he also sympathised with the owners who included the Dean and Chapter. In 1925 the Tory Henson praised the miners but condemned their leaders for urging a strike. The annual Miners' Gala in Durham City gave rise to an incident still remembered when I was in Durham 30 years later. Some miners saw a cleric in gaiters near the river and attempted to throw him in.[3] Minus top hat and umbrella, the cleric who was rescued turned out to be the Dean, who was 6ft 5ins, with a 63ins waist and a tiny voice. He had a 'rollicking gait' and Henson later called him *rhinobottomus* – the young Princess Elizabeth had told Henson she had seen one at the zoo.

Henson collapsed whilst preaching in March 1926. A doctor said that his poisoned gums meant that all his teeth should be removed. This happened and the bishop found false teeth 'the most disgusting experience'.[4]

He disliked Lang, and when he commented that a recent painting portrayed him as 'proud, arrogant and worldly', Henson said 'To which of these attributes does your Grace take exception?'[5]

---

[3] Some say that they succeeded.
[4] Owen Chadwick, *Hensley Henson* (1983), pp. 158 – 166.
[5] Probably this was Sir William Orpen's portrait painted in 1924.

Illness brought him down during the General Strike, and he found it difficult to say anything meaningful. He retired in 1938 and died in 1947 at Hintlesham in Suffolk.

Postscript by the Revd Richard Coles

I am a priest because I saw others make it look possible. First was the Rector of the village where we lived when I was growing up, Freddie Whittle. He was blind and lived alone in the Rectory where I would see him sometimes moving around in darkness at night, having no need of light. He came to lunch one day and unthinkingly I hummed under my breath the passage in Peter Grimes when the townspeople greet the Rector, 'good mor-or-ning, good mor-or-ning, good mooooor-ning!' Freddie said 'Peter Grimes', and I realised I was not the only Britten fan in Great Addington. Freddie introduced me as teenager to a world of culture – books, music, theatre – and changed the course of my life.

Later, it was John Gaskell, Vicar of St Alban's Holborn, who made it look possible. In spite of his fierce Anglo–Catholic appearance he was a patient and loving priest and a brilliant teacher, whose preaching delighted John Betjeman and Princess Margaret as well as those of us who were lucky enough to hear him Sunday by Sunday in the pews. John not only opened up for me the mysteries of the Christian religion but also made me see it could be possible to be a Christian without sacrificing too much of integrity or authenticity, without becoming either invisible or preposterous (others may think, if not invisible, I am most certainly preposterous, and if so, *mea culpa*).

Both Freddie and John would, I think, have appealed to the caricaturists Malcolm Johnson has so skilfully recovered from the magazine rack of history. Like many of those within they were halfway to caricatures themselves, but by that I do not mean in any way fake; rather, they looked like what you thought they should look like, as suited to their callings as the characters in Happy Families. Freddie – tall, with long grey hair swept back, like Peter Cushing in a Dracula film – declined to wear dark glasses and his sightless eyes made children stare and the rest of us wonder quite where to look when we were talking to him. John, bald and beaky in a black biretta with a scarlet pom, peered at the world through frameless glasses so thick they made his eyes too tiny for his face. He was Vicar of St Alban's Holborn, whose first vicar, the tragic Father Mackonochie, is caricatured by Ape in this book.

Both looked like parsons, hardly a merit you may think, but in an age when clergy seem determined not to look like clergy, eschewing the collar and sober black, or clerical dress altogether, I feel a great nostalgia for a time when bishops' aprons and deans' rosettes were worn with as much propriety as a guardsman his bearskin and a matron her cape. This is not antiquarianism, or not entirely, but a nostalgia for an age when clergy took their places much more confidently in the world than today.

In this book we see them take their place alongside the great statesmen of the day, the Lords Salisbury and Russell and Beaconsfield, literally their peers in the cases of Temple and King and Cosmo Gordon Lang, whose influence and indeed power shaped the Victorian world.

Less influential perhaps, but no less picturesque, are the eccentrics, Mrs Star, of whom I knew nothing, the former Mother Superior of a convent in Hull taken to court by another sister for ill treatment. In Ape's caricature, in her habit and in the dock, she looks downright sinister, though that may just be a reaction to hearing she was to be fined a fortune. I have heard of Fr Ignatius, however, who affected the habit of a Benedictine monk, received a highly suspect ordination at the hands of Syrian Metropolitan, and founded a community at Llanthony in the Black Mountains where he was dogged by scandal until he died.

What would the caricaturists make of Malcolm Johnson? He was certainly not lacking in the confidence to take his place in the world, and did so with style and commitment, as the Rector of St Botolph's Aldgate, where I volunteered (for about five minutes) and saw at first-hand what a gospel in action might look like. He was certainly not lacking in courage; his commitment to justice for LGBT people in the church and in wider society was, and is, unflinching, even when the machinery of ecclesiastical censure ground into gear, as it so often did with the subjects of this book. And he looks like a clergyman too, he has the nose for it and the forehead, and a scarlet cassock and the hood of a Lambeth MA.

But I would include Malcolm with Freddie and John as a priest who simply made it look possible; not only priesthood but membership for the church, for me, for many. So *deo gratias*, Malcolm, and *ad multos annos*.

THE REVD RICHARD COLES
Parish Priest, St Mary the Virgin, Finedon

Bibliography

Aronson, Theo, *The King in Love* (John Murray 1988).

Batchelor, John, *Tennyson* (Chatto 2012).

Benson, A. C. and Viscount Esher, *Letters of Queen Victoria* Three Series (John Murray 1908).

Benson, A.C., *Edward White Benson* (Macmillan 1899).

Best, G.F.A., *Temporal Pillars* (Cambridge University Press 1964).

   Shaftesbury (Batsford 1964).

Bolt, Rodney, *As Good as God, as Clever as the Devil* (Atlantic Books 2011).

Bonham Carter, V., *Winston Churchill as I Knew Him* (Eyre and Spottiswoode 1965).

Calder-Marshall, Arthur, *The Enthusiast* (Faber 1962).

Carlyle, Thomas, *Reminiscences* (Oxford World's Classics 2000).

Carpenter, Edward, *Cantuar – The Archbishops in their Office* (Cassell 1971).

   (ed.) *House of Kings* (John Baker 1966).

Carpenter, S. C., *Church and People, 1789–1889* (SPCK 1933).

   Winnington-Ingram (Hodder and Stoughton 1949).

Chadwick, Owen, *The Victorian Church* Parts 1 and 2 (A. and C. Black 1966).

   Hensley Henson (Oxford University Press 1983).

Chandler, M., *Life of Liddon* (Gracewing 2000).

Chitty, Susan, *The Beast and the Monk* (Hodder and Stoughton1974).

Davidson, Randall and Benham, William, *Archibald Campbell Tait* 2 vols (Macmillan 1891).

Elton, Lord, *Edward King and our Times* (Bles 1958).

Ffinch, M., *G.K. Chesterton: A Biography,* (Harper Collins 1986).

Bibliography

Glendinning, Victoria, *Trollope* (Hutchinson 1992).

Gray, Robert, *Cardinal Manning* (Weidenfeld and Nicolson 1985).

Hayter, W., *Spooner* (W. H. Allen 1977).

Healey, Edna, *Lady Unknown: The Life of Angela Burdett-Coutts* (Sidgwick and Jackson1978).

Henson, H.H., *Retrospect of an Unimportant Life* (Oxford University Press 1942).

Hibbert, Christopher, *Disraeli: A Personal Memoir* (Harper Collins 2004).

Queen Victoria (Harper Collins 2000).

Jeal, Tim, *Baden Powell* (Hutchinson 1989).

Jenkins, Roy, *Gladstone* (Macmillan 1995).

Churchill (Macmillan 2001).

Johnson, Malcolm, *Bustling Intermeddler? Life of Bishop Charles James Blomfield* (Gracewing 2001).

Keene, Derek, Burns, Arthur and Saint, Andrew, (eds.) *St Paul's: The Cathedral Church of London 606–2004* (Yale 2004).

Liddon, H.P., *The Life of Edward Bouverie Pusey* 4 vols (1893–7).

Lockhart, J.G., *Cosmo Gordon Lang* (Hodder and Stoughton 1949).

Longford, Elizabeth, *Victoria R.I.* (Weidenfeld and Nicolson 1964).

Magnus, Philip, *King Edward the Seventh* (John Murray 1964).

Matthews, R. T. and Mellini, Peter, *In 'Vanity Fair'* (Scolar Press 1982).

Meacham, Standish, *Lord Bishop, The Life of Samuel Wilberforce* (Harvard 1970).

Newsome, David, *On the Edge of Paradise* (John Murray 1980).

The Convert Cardinals (John Murray 1993).

The Parting of Friends (John Murray 1966).

The Victorian World Picture (John Murray 1997).

Newton, John, *Search for a Saint: Edward King* (Epworth 1977).

Nutting, Anthony, *Gordon: Martyr and Misfit* (Constable1966).

Palmer, Bernard, *High and Mitred* (SPCK 1992).

Reverend Rebels (Darton, Longman &Todd 1993).

Parsons, Brian, *Committed to the Cleansing Flame* (Spire Books 2005).

Pearson, Hesketh, *The Smith of Smiths* (Faber and Faber 1934).

Prestige, G. L., *St Paul's in its Glory* (SPCK 1955).

Prestige, Leonard, *Pusey* (Mowbray, 1982).

Prothero, G. Rowland, *The Life and Correspondence of Arthur Penrhyn Stanley* 2 vols (John Murray 1894).

Reynolds, Michael, *Martyr of Ritualism: Father Mackonochie of St Alban's, Holborn* (Faber 1965).

Roberts, Andrew, *Salisbury* (Weidenfeld and Nicolson 1999).

Russell, G.W.E., *Edward King* (Smith, Elder1912).

St Aubyn, Giles, *Edward VII: Prince and King* (Collins 1979).

Stephenson, Alan, *The Victorian Archbishops of Canterbury* (Rocket Press 1991).

Strachey, Lytton, *Eminent Victorians* (Putnam 1918).

   Queen Victoria (Chatto and Windus1921).

Tallack, William, *Reminiscences of Edmund Sturge* (1905).

Ward, Leslie, *Forty Years of 'Spy'* (Chatto and Windus 1915).

Weintraub, S., *Disraeli* (Hamish Hamilton 1993).

Williams, David, *Genesis and Exodus: A Portrait of the Benson Family* (Hamish Hamilton 1979).

Wilson, A.N., *The Victorians* (Hutchinson 2002).

Witheridge, John, *Excellent Dr Stanley* (Michael Russell 2013).